P9-ARC-732
MARBORO

# ARENA

## THE STORY OF THE COLOSSEUM

*On the half-title:* Bronze sestertius of the Emperor Titus showing the Colosseum.

*Frontispiece:* 'As long as the Colosseum stands, so does Rome. When it falls, Rome falls and the whole world with it.'

JOHN PEARSON

# ARENA

## THE STORY OF THE COLOSSEUM

*with 151 black-and-white illustrations*

*McGRAW-HILL BOOK COMPANY*
*New York St. Louis San Francisco Toronto*

Etching of the Colosseum by Piranesi.

*for*
*Nancy Lüscher*

**Library of Congress Cataloging in Publication Data**

Pearson, John, 1930– Arena: the story of the Colosseum.

1. Rome (City) Colosseum – History. I. Title.
DG68.1.P4 913.37′6 73-6766
ISBN 0-07-049031-7

Printed and bound in Great Britain
by Jarrold and Sons Ltd, Norwich

# Contents

Coin showing the symbolic deification of the Emperor Vespasian.

# I The Emperor's Hundred Days

In the year AD 80 the Colosseum opened with what must stand as quite the longest, most disgusting, organized mass binge in history. According to Suetonius, various sorts of large-scale slaughter, both of animals and of men, were appreciatively watched by the Emperor Titus and a packed audience for the next hundred days. All this was considered highly laudable, an extra-special celebration of the state, duly enhanced by the presence of Roman senators, court officials, priests, vestal virgins and sacred effigies of the gods. The Emperor Titus was quite happily footing the enormous bill, just as he and his father, the imperial Vespasian, had already footed the bill for building this vast arena. Such payments were the privilege of power; the new arena was officially the gift of the Emperor to the Roman people and would ensure his fame for ever.

Not that this worked. Officially the arena was called the Flavian Amphitheatre, after the dynastic name of the Emperor, but several centuries ahead it would pick up its simpler and more lasting title. Ironically this name, which would erase all mention of the Flavians from popular memory, had originated with their hated predecessor, Nero. His colossal statue stood near the site of the arena. Rather than demolish it, Vespasian had ingeniously changed its head and its identity to that of Apollo, the sun god. And it was this colossus, with Apollo's head, but built by Nero, that gave the arena its enduring name, the Colosseum.

The opening was a delirious affair, a mammoth celebration on the grandest scale. For something like six years Rome's citizens had watched an army of skilled workmen draining the lake of Nero's Golden House which occupied the site, preparing the immense foundations, then raising the walls. All this had

Processions were something of a Roman speciality. Representation of an imperial triumph by Andrea Mantegna, the Renaissance artist who drew inspiration from his studies of antiquity.

started in the reign of Vespasian. That stingy but impressive Emperor was rebuilding Rome after the ravages of Nero's fire. He was determined that his city should recover its ancient splendour as the world's capital; the Colosseum, more than any other building, symbolized the massiveness, the power and sense of order of the new régime. One of the last acts of Vespasian's life was to dedicate it, proudly, in the year AD 79.

Titus succeeded him and piously continued work on the arena. From the scant evidence of the historians, Titus appears to have been one of the kindliest men to rule Rome. He is the emperor Suetonius describes complaining over supper of not having had a chance to do anyone a favour since the previous day. 'My friends,' the Emperor exclaimed, 'I have wasted a day.' And yet this kindly man shared his father's passion for the arena. Work on the Colosseum had been hurried on, and he clearly could not wait for the shows to start. As it was, the Colosseum was not completely finished for these celebrations; its fourth and final storey was to be added in the reign of the next Emperor, the unspeakable Domitian, last of the Flavians.

Despite this, Titus had lavished money on it. It was a show-piece, and must already have possessed something today's bare ruins make it hard to picture – a sense of ostentatious luxury. This was a vulgar age. Imperial Rome rejoiced in over-decoration and extravagance. The outside walls of the amphi-theatre were plastered over the stonework, disguising the construction, niches were adorned with statues of the gods, the ceilings of the seventy-two public stairways were painted gold and purple, all inside walls were faced with marble.

Before this opening day, the audience had been well primed with advance publicity – still further evidence that the occasion was regarded as a full-scale act of state. This build-up was important. Titus, like all successful Roman emperors, took his public relations seriously. The day had been proclaimed a public holiday. For weeks past there had been posters and announce-ments daubed on the walls of public buildings giving the names of star performers taking part, along with all the different spectacles offered by the Emperor's generosity. On the actual day programmes were on sale. To make the opening more impressive still, Titus was set to make this an imperial festival. Suddenly Rome was full of foreigners, many invited from the furthest corners of the Empire and beyond. Rome could feel itself the centre of the world.

The poet Martial, faithfully echoing the official line, made much of this in flattering verses to the Emperor. 'Where do

The Emperor Vespasian (69–79), obstinate, methodical and realistic, and (*right*) his highly popular son, the Emperor Titus (79–81), provider of the inaugural games in the Colosseum.

such people come from, Caesar, with the whole world now crammed into your city?' Offhand he named a few – the visitors from Rhodes, from Anatolia and from the upper reaches of the Nile, Arabs, Sabaean horsemen from Arabia Felix, pig-tailed Sicambrians, Abyssinians with matted hair – 'all come to honour Caesar as their Lord'.

The mood is reminiscent of Victorian England in its imperial heyday, with citizens of every corner of the Empire visiting London for the 1897 Jubilee. And this was very much the key-note of the opening ceremony, the Empire and the city honouring the Emperor. His approach was staged like a triumphal march, and for the audience the first they heard would have been the roar of the crowds outside as they caught sight of the imperial procession advancing down the Via Sacra.

Processions always had been something of a Roman speciality, a method of uniting the city in the excitement of a general's triumph, along with all the dignity of priests, gods and the Roman Senate. Since Caesar's triumph after his Gallic Wars, the staging had grown steadily more elaborate. In a pre-cinematic age, this was an unrivalled way of demonstrating one man's power and splendour to the greatest number, of imposing image upon ascending image of the emperor's grandeur.

The tradition of the Roman triumph dates back to the Republic. The triumph of Sosius, from the frieze of the Temple of Apollo, first century BC.

All the same, this procession of the Emperor Titus does seem a curious and tasteless hotch-potch. Its very incongruity offers a glimpse of the discordant elements within the emperor's power. First came the emphasis on pure tradition – the lictors, who from the days of the Republic had been the guardians of the consuls, bearing the *fasces*, the bound rods, symbol of their authority. Then followed a contingent of young boys, all of good family, specially chosen, according to Dionysius, 'so that the foreigners might freely see the flower of the city's youth, how fine and numerous they were'. Knights' sons rode horse-back, the remainder marched. Then there were charioteers, then athletes. They introduced the gladiators, led by the *andabati*, mounted fighters, riding white Roman chargers, who in their turn were followed by fighting men, each in their different groups and with their different uniforms; *retiarii* with nets and tridents, and swordsmen with their plumes and their resplendent armour. The heaviest of all, the *hoplomachi*, were enormous men covered in armour and carrying the big curved shields of the legionaries. They had killed many men in the arena. They were a race apart, the Empire's licensed murderers. They had a key place in the procession: their presence must have brought a dark excitement to these celebrations.

An African elephant, as it appears on a silver double shekel, *c.* 220 BC.

When they had plodded past, the procession suddenly changed character again. These switches were a speciality of Rome's showmen. After the killers it was time for light relief, the circus turns that everybody loved. Ever since Julius Caesar had ridden in triumph to the Capitol on an elephant, elephants were *de rigeur* in any big procession worthy of its name. Better than any other creature they expressed the Roman virtues – size, splendour, discipline. They might have been specially designed for the Colosseum, and the procession had full-grown African elephants, with their trainers. Later the animals would be put to fight in the arena, matched against bears, lions, leopards and hunters from North Africa who killed them in the

Roman musicians, dancers and a dwarf on a mosaic from the Aventine.

wild. But these were tame. So were the other animals that followed – cheetahs, gazelles, elkhounds from Ireland, long-haired buffalo.

After the animals, dancers – some of them grown men, some boys, some adolescent youths – dancing the pagan dances of antiquity accompanied by lyre-players. The men wore purple tunics, heavy bronze belts and carried swords and lances. In their own way they were a splendid sight, a sort of military ballet acting the warlike movements of the Pyrrhic dance.

By now the procession was approaching its crescendo. At this point, incense was burned, pipes played as Rome's altars were carried past, followed by the priesthood – the flamens crowned with vines, the college of the priests and finally the vestal virgins, veiled and seated in their sacred carriage. Following them came effigies of gods, attended by young girls scattering flowers – Mars and Diana, Jupiter and Juno, Neptune and Minerva. Heaven, like Rome, was overcrowded. The city had twelve tutelary deities. Each was entitled to his part in the parade. So were their offspring, and all demi-gods associated with the city – nymphs, muses, graces, Bacchus and Hercules, the deified emperors. Then came the climax of the whole procession, high priest and emperor, 'beloved and delight of the whole world', the Emperor Titus Flavius.

An emperor's triumph became symbolic of the power of the Empire. Relief showing the triumph of Titus from the Arch of Titus.

*Venationes* (hunts) were another traditional Roman pastime which became formalized in the arena. Hunting in the wild as depicted on a mosaic at Lillebonne.

Still barely forty, handsome and gracious, stormer of the city of Jerusalem, reformed rake and favourite of the soldiers, fluent in Greek as well as Latin, equally adept in the arts of war and peace, Titus, like the young Henry VIII of England, had inherited a throne made safe and wealthy by a frugal father. When he was carried into the Colosseum in his imperial litter, the applause that greeted him was deafening. Tradition prescribed the greeting, the entire audience rising, waving their handkerchiefs, applauding 'like thunder in a storm'. Within this enormous echo-chamber the effect would have been overwhelming. Amid the acclamations he mounted the podium to return the people's greetings. They shouted back their wishes for long life, a happy reign, and in this atmosphere of supercharged good-will the Emperor ordered the show to start. The Colosseum opened. It was to stay open for four hundred years; and when it closed the Roman Empire had fallen. So had unnumbered animals and men in the arena.

According to Dio Cassius the performance started with the sort of multiple extravaganza the Romans loved. However cultured and good-natured Titus may have been in private, he was relying here on cruelty, vulgarity and sheer excess. He was quite clearly out to sate the public's gluttony for blood. He must have ransacked the whole Roman repertoire. Nothing was omitted that might titillate, excite and satisfy the lowest instincts of the mob. For the next hundred days the arena saw a public holocaust.

First there was carnage, a mass slaughter of wild animals to put everyone in good humour, a whole zoo loosed into the arena, then hunted down. This was performed by *bestiarii*, specially trained showmen-hunters who took on lions, bears, leopards, in hand-to-hand combat. Often men were killed, especially as the beasts were usually maddened by thirst and hunger when they appeared. The audience relished this, preferring massed effects to single combat like a modern bullfight – whole groups of lion suddenly released upon a dozen hunters, a hunting tableau with the arena set with trees and boulders, round which the hunters chased cranes, antelope, hyenas and gazelles.

The audience had grown to expect the occasional special effect, such as a wrestling match with crocodiles or the slow killing of a full-grown lion with a gilded mane. But what they really liked was quantity – a plethora of deaths. This was what Titus gave them. There was a sort of negligent largesse about the way these beautiful rare creatures were expended. As evidence of the Emperor's generosity, Suetonius mentions that five thousand animals were slaughtered in a single day. These included several of the elephants that marched past in the procession. Elephants always were a popular item on the agenda. The only death the audience preferred was human death. It duly followed.

A *venatio* in the arena, from a fourth-century mosaic now in the Villa Borghese, Rome.

Incidental entertainment at the fights was provided by musicians. The mosaic (*below*), from the Roman villa at Nennig, shows a water-organ and a horn-player.

(*Right*) a *hoplomachus* from Ephesus in Asia Minor.

There was a pause as slaves cleared the arena. They finished off the animals that still showed signs of life, then dragged the bodies outside to be slung into deep pits, *carnaria*, which had been dug on waste land near the Colosseum. (When, eighteen hundred years later, the archaeologist Lanciani excavated several of these pits, the filth and stench still overwhelmed his hardiest workmen.) The arena cleared, black slaves spread fresh sand and raked it carefully. Such minutiae of gamesmanship were scrupulously observed. While this was going on there was a lull. The audience chatted, waved to each other, watched the Emperor and his favourites for anything that could be turned into a spot of gossip. According to Ovid, this was the ideal moment to pick up a girl by asking to look at her programme. Then, before the audience became impatient, there was a blare of horns and tubas from below the podium. This heralded the gladiators.

On this first day before the Emperor, they would have been

(*Below*) gladiatorial combat in a training school between a *retiarius* and a lightly armed *myrmillo*. The contest is being overseen by a trainer.

(*Right*) bronze statuette of a gladiator.

professionals, proud men and well-trained fighters, the flower of the gladiator schools, hand-picked for the occasion. And as they marched into the arena they must have made a most impressive sight, superbly dressed in armour, plumes and sumptuous cloaks, provided by the Emperor. They marched in strictest precedence, while the crowd roared and the orchestra played martial music. Each type of gladiator formed something of a team, each with its uniform, its style of fighting and its supporters in the audience. The giant *hoplomachi* would move slowly and rely on armour and brute strength. The lighter-armoured men were known as 'Thracians', after their Greek-style dress and their small circular Grecian shields. In combat they used agility and speed against the *hoplomachi*. Then came the *retiarii*, the net-fighters. These had virtually no armour and tried to entangle their lumbering opponents in their net before transfixing them with their tridents. *Retiarii* ranked below the other types of gladiator and had the shortest life-span.

These were the three classic types of gladiator, and each group had a distinct *esprit de corps* among themselves. Their supporters cheered them on, booed their opponents, bet on their chances. Even the Emperor was involved in this. Titus was known to be a Thracian man, just as Domitian was a determined fan of the *hoplomachi*. And Marcus Aurelius, one of the few emperors who wanted nothing to do with the arena, wrote quite explicitly that he could not be bothered to support 'either the lights or the heavies'.

To demonstrate that this particular show was something special, Titus had provided the unusual luxury of mounted fighters, the *andabati* who led the gladiators in the procession – he also gave a group of charioteers. Charioteer-gladiators were an innovation of Julius Caesar's after his campaign in Britain, and were considered a great treat by the audience.

Before the fighting could begin, one further piece of ritual had still to be observed. The Emperor had to show his unmistakable involvement in all that followed and lend imperial dignity to the fighting. The gladiators' deaths would then be his responsibility, just as the combats were a state event.

The parade of gladiators lined up beneath the podium, then in the hush that followed the men gave the traditional grim greeting to the Emperor – 'We who are about to die salute you.' The Emperor solemnly acknowledged this; then, as official donor of the show, he had the duty of testing the sharpness of the weapons. This ceremony, the *probatio armorum*, was customary before all gladiatorial fights, and was not just symbolic. If the swords were inadequate to kill, he could be held at fault. Domitian had used the occasion to insist on sharper swords for his gladiators. So did Tiberius' son, Drusus, who had one particularly lethal type of gladiator's sword named after him.

It would be pointless to deny the hideous excitement of what followed. A passage in the *Confessions* of St Augustine shows something of the frightening fascination of the gladiatorial show and how contagious the blood lust of the audience could be. He tells how one of his followers, a Christian called Alypius, is taken to the arena, much against his will, by friends.

When they arrived at the arena the place was seething with the lust for cruelty. They found seats as best they could and Alypius shut his eyes tightly, determined to have nothing to do with these atrocities. If only he had closed his ears as well! For an incident in the fight drew a great roar from the crowd, and this thrilled him so deeply that he could not contain his curiosity. Whatever had caused the uproar, he was confident that, if he saw it, he would find it repulsive and remain master of himself. So he opened his eyes and his soul was stabbed with a wound more deadly than any which the gladiator, whom he was so anxious to see, had received in his body. . . . When he saw the blood, it was as though he had drunk a deep draught of savage passion. Instead of turning away, he fixed his eyes on the scene and drank in all its frenzy.

That first day in the Colosseum the 'great roar from the crowd' must have arisen time and again once the fighting started. Everything imaginable was done to enhance this mass excitement. The combats opened to the blood-curdling blare of Roman war-trumpets; as the fights developed, the musicians below the Emperor's box egged on the crowd with fierce background music.

As with the slaughter of the animals, the emphasis here was on variety and quantity. The ideal seems to have been to make the arena a battlefield in miniature, and gladiators fought in groups – lights against heavies, an interlude for chariot-fights, a dozen *hoplomachi* seemingly surrounded by *retiarii.* Staging and over-all effect counted for more than any individual performance; as fast as men were killed, others were hurried on to take their place. The impression was of a surging game of death, the immense audience worked up to near-hysteria and willing the protagonists to acts of futile courage and annihilation.

In lesser shows, the fighting was often little more than licensed butchery as well-armed gladiators destroyed their inexperienced opponents. Such victims were mob-fodder – condemned criminals, war prisoners or fugitives from slavery. Here it was different. Thanks to the importance of the show, well-proven gladiators were matched against each other. Some would have been popular heroes with reputations to sustain. All would have been in peak of health, meticulously armed and trained as thoroughly as present-day professional sportsmen.

This ensured some show of virtuosity in combat. There was an elaborate *corpus* of gladiatorial lore taught in the schools and understood by the *aficionados* of the ring. For the swordsman, style was as important as for a modern matador. Particular gladiators were famous for the speed of their attack, their cunning in defence, their great physique. Their portraits were painted for their public, some even had admirers rich enough to commission pictures of them in mosaic, so that we can still see their bovine features and exaggerated muscles.

Four heroes of the Roman arena. Aldous Huxley said of them that they were 'filled with the essence of Roman reality'. (*Below*) the reality of the arena vividly recalled on a fourth-century mosaic, now in the Villa Borghese.

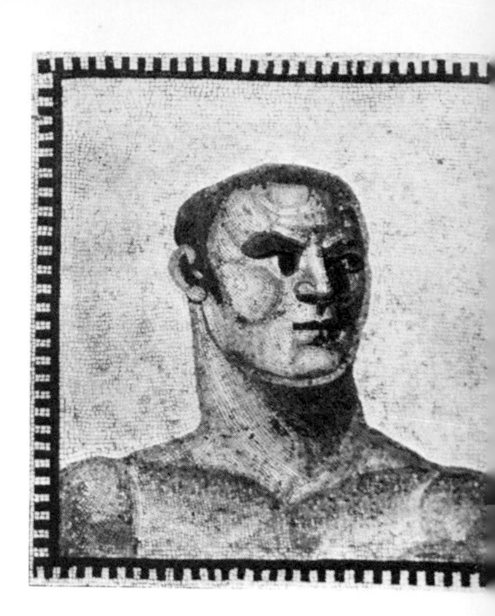

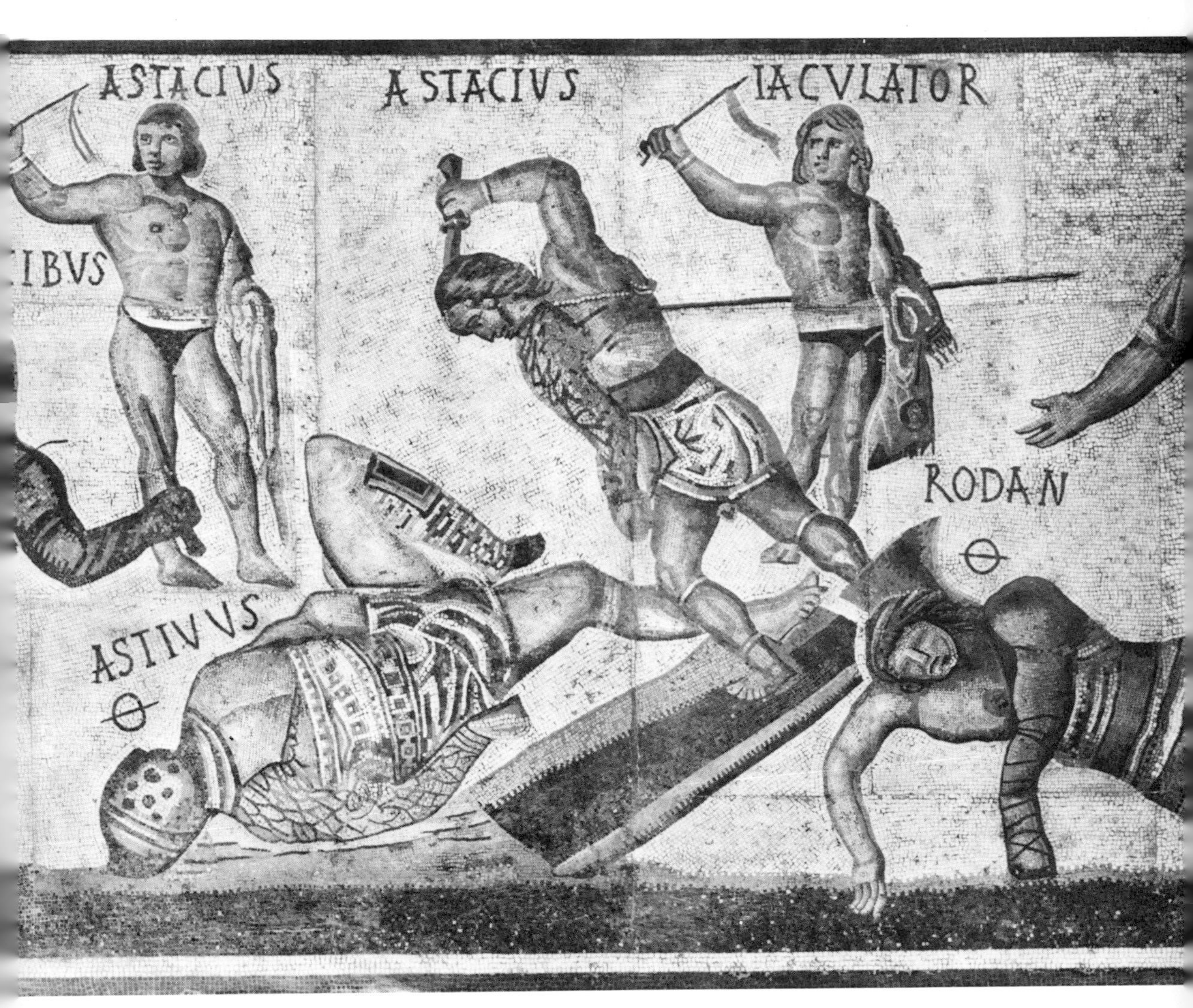
ASTACIVS
ASTACIVS
IACVLATOR
IBVS
RODAN
ASTIVVS

Gladiators became a popular theme for everyday Roman decoration. On this lamp a *myrmillo* prepares the death-blow for his defeated adversary.

With such a cult of personality surrounding them, the star gladiators Titus had engaged must have been on their mettle from the start. They were performers with a demanding audience. But they were something more. They were quite simply fighting for their lives, and this produced a savagery, an understandable involvement in their performance beyond mere obligations to the Emperor or the audience.

As the gladiators closed with one another, their supporters cheered them on with what Professor Grant calls 'training manual slogans', like crowds at any modern boxing match. Each cut and parry was appreciated. Style counted. But the real climax everybody wanted was an effective hit, the final knock-out blow or thrust that laid one gladiator at the mercy of his opponent. By the rules of the arena, this was the crowd's moment.

The trumpets sounded, halting the action. The spectators roared out – 'Got him! He's had it!' And while the victorious gladiator stood with his sword ready, his opponent dropped his shield and raised one finger of his left hand in the traditional plea for mercy. In theory this was for Titus to decide. He was the giver of the show. But in practice it was the spectators who decided the fate of the fallen. If they were feeling sentimental, if the poor wretch had fought well, shown spirit, or for some reason pleased the crowd, the majority could still be in his favour. Thumbs would go up; there would be cheers for him, waved handkerchiefs, and the Emperor would graciously offer him his life. But if the audience were feeling mean, if they felt that the man had fought badly, had shown too much regard for his own safety, if they were simply in the mood for blood, their thumbs would turn down. The Emperor would confirm their verdict, and the victorious gladiator had the task of finishing his rival.

Even here the conventions were observed. Part of the gladiator's job was to die decently; during his training he would have learned that it was bad form in a properly trained gladiator to make a fuss of death. Equally, his victor was expected to help by dispatching him efficiently.

This cult of dying was important. By observing the conventions, even through the final agony of death, the gladiator gave the killing an air of spurious dignity. Serious supporters of the arena often seized on this moment in an attempt to justify the sport, rather like those today who urge that foxes must enjoy the hunt.

Everything proceeded now according to the strictest ritual. The defeated gladiator, granted his reprieve, was permitted to limp off through a special gate, the Porta Sanavivaria. The dead were dealt with by arena slaves dressed up as Charun, the traditional death demon of the Etruscans. They wore horns and black livery and used the hammers of the Etruscan devils to make sure the defeated men were truly dead. When they had done their work, the bodies were dragged out with grappling-hooks by further slaves, this time dressed up as Mercury, the mythical conductor of dead souls to hell. It was all carefully arranged to form a parody of death. The bodies were dragged through the Porta Libitinensis, named after Libitina, goddess of burials. Then in a special room, the *spoliarium*, they were efficiently stripped of their armour, which was repaired, cleaned and returned to stores, unless somebody were smart enough to grab a souvenir beforehand. Relics from dead gladiators were in demand. The bride whose hair was parted with a defeated gladiator's spear was said to be sure of marital good fortune. The blood of freshly slaughtered gladiators was a specific against impotence and infecundity. An item of their clothing warded off the evil eye.

Just occasionally defeated gladiators would be discovered still alive when they were stripped. The slaves would cut their throats. Sometimes the dead men would have relatives or comrades to give their bodies decent burial. The Emperor Caracalla once ordered the gladiator Bato to fight three successive duels in a day; when he was killed the Emperor gave his remains a splendid funeral. Bato was someone special. It was rare for an emperor to worry where a gladiator was buried. If no one claimed the body after a show, it was thrown into the *carnaria* along with dead animals and other refuse.

Meanwhile the victors could enjoy their brief glory. The heralds' trumpets announced the end of the fighting. The ring was carefully re-sanded. Amid wild applause from the multitude, the Emperor solemnly presented the successful gladiators with, of all things, palm branches, symbolizing victory. Some famous gladiators picked up dozens of these ghoulish souvenirs before their time arrived to garnish someone else's reputation. As well as honour there was money for the victors, paid out in ready cash by the imperial hand. Amounts were generous and set out in contracts made before the show. The emperors were meticulous about money.

A gladiator floored by his opponent.

Normally, this would have been the end of the day's entertainment – for Titus it was only the beginning. Just as the crowd was preparing to leave, the arena filled with water. In came horses and performing bulls, specially trained to work in water.

Before the crowd got over its surprise, the animals were followed by small ships, each manned by gladiators dressed as sailors. The ships went into action, and the gladiators acted out the classic bloody naval battle between Corinth and Corfu. Many were killed – no Roman audience can have enjoyed quite so much action in a single day.

This was only the beginning. The next day's festivities were wilder than ever. Not even the Colosseum was big enough for everything the Emperor had in mind, and Titus turned to the huge artificial lake Augustus had constructed eighty years before beside the Tiber. Here Titus gave his city-dwellers a spectacle which few can have ever seen – a full-scale naval battle with proper ships manned by slaves, prisoners-of-war and criminals. This was a great success among the vast crowd thronging the banks. The performers were all fighting for their lives; countless among them died. Ships were rammed, boarded, set on fire and sunk. But once again Titus appears to have known his audience. Rather than risk boring them, he gave an order and the lake was quickly drained. The debris of the naval fight was cleared away, and then the basin of the lake was made the scene for another massed gladiator show and an enormous slaughtering of animals.

From then on the Emperor Titus must have been caught up in a frenzy of excess, strange in so outwardly sane a man, one of those surrealistic orgies in which certain rulers became obsessed with proving the limitlessness of their power. There was another naval battle, followed by a full-scale assault by infantry and cavalry on a mock-town specially built in the Circus Maximus. There were more hunts, more shows of gladiators, pageants and pantomimes and circus shows, chariot-races, plays and hunting scenes and massacres. Inside the Colosseum something was always going on. Rome had become, in Lewis Mumford's memorable phrase, 'one vast collective torture chamber'.

Bullfighters from Thessaly showed how they played the bulls, leapt barefoot on their backs, and killed them by wrestling with their horns and breaking their necks. Sometimes the men were killed. There were the vast set-pieces that the Romans loved – the arena would be planted with trees or set with fountains. It would become a forest or a desert or a lake. Choirs performed; so did dancers, acrobats and actors. Sometimes the shows were held at night, the Colosseum lit by oil-flares. The next emperor devised a massive chandelier of iron which was lowered into the arena for these late-night shows.

But unlike some showmen, the Emperor Titus appears never

to have neglected the ordinary citizens. There must have been times when even the Roman appetite for blood and spectacle began to wilt. When this happened he arranged impromptu give-away events which foreshadow modern television shows. Small wooden balls would shower upon the audience. Some of the balls were empty, others contained official chits for sums of money, horses, chickens and even for whole houses. (During the next reign Domitian went one further, livening up the Colosseum's audience with a sudden shower of gold coins, *glacé* fruit and Numidian partridges.)

Once one attempts to understand what all this meant in terms of human lives, of effort and resources, Titus' Hundred Days appear as one of the most extraordinary 'happenings' in history. Not until Hollywood had any single man made quite such massive and inhuman efforts to preserve his fellow men from boredom. The sheer expenditure of money, life and energy, the planning, engineering skill and organization lavished upon these shows were of the order of a full-scale military campaign. But instead of fighting an enemy, kindly Titus chose to pour a torrent of blood and treasure into the most appalling party of all time – all this to celebrate the construction of a building that linked public sadism with government, and made licensed butchery the one popular expression of the Roman genius.

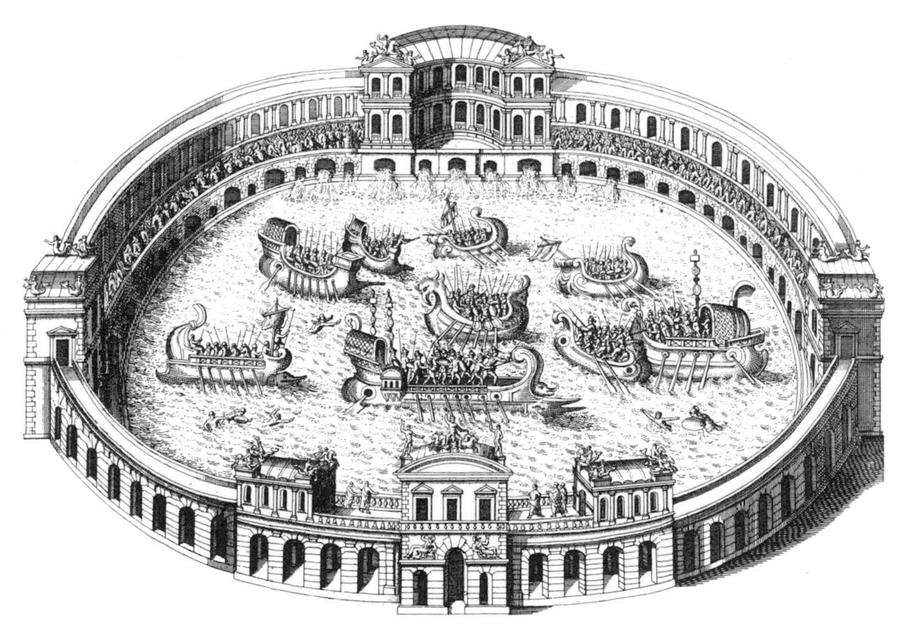

Renaissance portrayal of a *naumachia*, a naval battle staged within the flooded arena.

# II Origins

View of the Circus Maximus on a sestertius of the Emperor Trajan.

The Melanesians of the Pacific once disembowelled their most handsome captives of both sexes after a successful war as a thank-offering to the gods. Hottentots, devout Hindus and Stone Age Scandinavians have all been known to slaughter much-loved offspring to ward off divine anger during a famine or a drought. Even in the last century, respectable Brahmin ladies followed the practice of the early Mesopotamians, the Vikings and the Incas of Peru by sacrificing themselves at their husbands' funerals. And these first-century Romans sitting crammed on to the freshly cut stone seats of the Colosseum and bawling on their favourite gladiators were also taking part in something that undoubtedly began in prehistoric times as a most solemn form of human sacrifice.

Exactly why this happened is still something of a mystery. Indeed, the whole evolution of these extravagant and highly organized state death-spectacles is strange. In their development they would seem to have gone against the rules. Human sacrifice is widespread at a fairly primitive level of society, but as societies advance it generally dies out or becomes sublimated into some form of symbolic sacrifice. Animals or substitute figures take the place of people, and the early Romans had certainly left human sacrifice behind them in their religion. Both Livy and Plutarch refer to it disdainfully as an un-Roman practice. Livy records just one occasion, in the year 216 BC, when one of the vestal virgins, convicted of unchastity, was buried alive. In the same year two Gauls and two Greeks were also buried alive in the Forum Boarium, but Livy mentions this to emphasize how unusual such conduct was in Rome, and in the year 97 BC the Senate formally abolished human sacrifice. All that remained were obvious symbolic relics of such practices

Animals replaced human beings as sacrificial objects as early as the third century BC. This relief, dated about 40 BC, from the Temple of Neptune shows a bull about to be sacrificed.

– the straw figures thrown into the Tiber every spring, the animals still sacrificed upon the Capitol, the winning horse in the annual race to the Forum which was slain and its head exposed over its stables.

This makes it the more mysterious that, from the third century BC, gladiatorial combat, which started as a form of human sacrifice in honour of the dead, steadily grew more common and more cruel in Rome. The first recorded instance of such combat there took place between three pairs of gladiators in the Forum Boarium in the year 264 BC. It was staged in the cause of filial piety at the funeral of Brutus Perus and paid for by his sorrowing sons, Marcus and Decius. Between them they were both introducing a distinctly foreign practice into the mourning habits of the city. It had been consciously borrowed from the Romans' ancient enemies, the Etruscans. One would like to know exactly why such a barbarous and apparently alien idea gradually caught on in the centre of the civilized world.

Although it seems clear that gladiators were an Etruscan invention, here too their development is something of a mystery. The practice of such sophisticated fights to the death has no parallel among the death cults of other primitive religions and seems to have grown in popularity instead of disappearing as Etruscan civilization advanced. It originated with a form of battle sacrifice which occurred among the early peoples of the Mediterranean. Herodotus mentions the Scythians of ancient Thrace practising human sacrifice at the funerals of their warriors. The Carthaginians indulged in it as well. And Homer, in his account of the death of Patroclus, describes how prisoners were slaughtered to appease the shades of their dead enemies.

However repellent human sacrifice may be, there is often something touching in its logic – the idea that the gods possessed a right to even the most precious member of the family, the feeling that the dead are lonely and in need of company. Clearly the Etruscans shared such feelings. They were a people much concerned with death, and one of their obsessions was with ensuring that their dead were comfortable. Close to the sites of their important towns like Cervetri and Tarquinia one can still see signs of this obsession in their subterranean cemetery villages. The Etruscans had a genius for the homely tomb. Some of the rooms are sumptuously furnished, the walls painted with scenes of life – dancing and festivals and hunting and love-making. Largely from the evidence of these tomb-paintings, D. H. Lawrence built up his famous picture of the Etruscans as a spontaneous, life-worshipping people. What he failed to notice was the corollary of this – their heightened and exaggerated sense of death. For the Etruscans, death was a hateful parody of life, the hereafter the place where the departed were tormented by an atrocious sense of loss and jealousy for the living. In an attempt to ease this jealousy, the Etruscans seem to have devised the earliest gladiatorial combats to the death.

As the Marchese Scipio Maffei put it in his *Compleat History of the Ancient Amphitheatres*, published in London in 1730:

> A motive of Religion paved the way to this most celebrated Institution [of gladiators], namely that most ancient Opinion, that the souls of the deceased, who were in a manner deified by leaving the body, delighted in human blood, and that the slaughter of men by way of sacrifice in honour of them, rendered them propitious, or at least pleased, and their wrath appeased as if slain to satisfy their revenge.

And so, among the early Etruscans, concern for the dead demanded cruelty to the living. Spirits were clamouring for revenge. Piety demanded blood and suffering. To provide it the Etruscans took revenge just one step beyond ordinary sacrifice by making their victims kill each other.

There was an ancient precedent for this in the idea of forcing soldiers to kill their former comrades as an extreme punishment and a form of military disgrace. Among the Romans this was later to be known as *fustuarium*. According to Professor Lintott, 'when a military force had been routed or suffered similar disgrace it was divided into tens, and one man selected by lot from each of the ten was clubbed to death by his fellow soldiers'. Crassus adopted this technique with the disgraced soldiers who failed to deal with Spartacus and his gladiator army outside Naples; so did Apronius against the Romans who deserted against Tacfarinas. On Marcus Aurelius' Column, defeated German tribesmen are depicted killing one another as the accepted punishment for treachery. The ancient Etruscans presumably believed that their dead comrades would enjoy this final touch of horror in their battle sacrifices.

But with the Etruscans something beyond mere piety must have been involved in the development of the whole cult of gladiators. Concern for the dead was masking a keen sense of sadistic voyeurism among the living. Religion and revenge were an excuse for people to enjoy the spectacle of human butchery. And as the taste spread it was not long before the Etruscan genius for public festivals transformed this battle sacrifice of mourning into something of a spectator sport. This

The supreme punishment for a defeated enemy was to be forced to kill each other. In this relief from the column of Marcus Aurelius, German prisoners are seen executing their comrades.

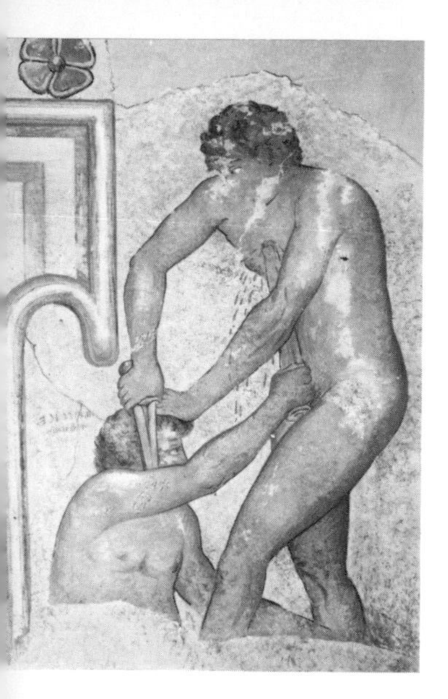

Mortal combat gradually assumed a central role in Etruscan death-rites. This tomb-painting portrays Polynice slaying Eteocles.

required time and some imagination but the development is clear. It was a short step to transfer these combats between prisoners from the battlefield to the funeral of any warrior or important citizen. Prisoners-of-war could be selected and preserved for such occasions. If prisoners were lacking, slaves would do just as well, provided they were burly, well trained and dressed for the part. Training meant fighting-schools. Schools in their turn began to turn out specially trained fighting men with a clear code of conduct and style of combat. The gladiator's craft had started.

Evidence of these Etruscan gladiators is scanty, but there is enough to show just how the craft developed. The Etruscans worked out all the essential principles of what was to become a Roman institution. A tomb-painting in Tarquinia shows an Etruscan gladiator whose dress and evident style of fighting might have belonged to one of the Roman *hoplomachi*. Engravings on Etruscan grave-*cistae* show that they dressed their gladiators in stylized versions of enemy uniforms, just as the Romans did, and had the dead dragged off by slaves disguised as the devil Charun. Combats took place in specially dug hollows in the earth, prefiguring the form of the full-scale Roman arena. And as well as the fights between gladiators, the Etruscans also staged hunts of wild beasts by specially trained hunters. In short, gladiatorial fighting was a complete and finished cult among the Etruscans when the trend-setting sons of Brutus Perus brought it to Rome.

This helps explain the apparently effortless way the practice then caught on among the wealthy Romans of the late third and early second centuries BC. The rules were all worked out, the fashion was established. And Romans, always reluctant innovators but great borrowers and exploiters of other men's ideas, adopted them as if they were a custom of their own city. No criticism, no public outcry is recorded. Perhaps this is because the combats, to begin with, were exclusively confined to funerals. Even in this the Romans copied the Etruscans. A rich Roman's funeral could be an impressive affair, a solemn demonstration of the family's prestige. Under this solemnity the gladiators quietly entered Rome.

There is no reason to suppose that the well-heeled sons of Brutus Perus were impelled by the bloodthirsty, demon-haunted credo of the Etruscans when they arranged for their six gladiators to fight it out in the Forum Boarium. It would have been extremely odd if, as educated Romans, they had believed that their dead father's shade was being comforted by the blood

Sacrifice of Trojan prisoners at Patroclus' funeral, part of the ritual attempt to appease the dead. Detail of a tomb-painting from Vulci.

of a few slaves slaughtered in his honour. But what their father certainly would have relished was the show, the interest it aroused among the citizens of Rome, the way it immediately got him and his family talked about. This was the reason why his sons made their historic innovation. Thanks to their initiative, gladiators were soon established as an impressive status symbol at a rich man's death. For a while, gladiators were known as *bustiarii* – funeral men.

As these bloodthirsty funeral junketings continued, Rome soon picked up a taste for them. Because of the expense they were still something of a rarity and were regarded rather as a treat for the common people paid for by their betters. Soon they were becoming more lavish and more frequent. In the year 216 BC Marcus Lepidus went to his ancestors, taking with him some of the forty-four gladiators who fought during his obsequies in the Forum. Sixteen years later, Marcus Valerius Levinus had 50 gladiators battling at his funeral. By 183 BC Publius Licinius was being honoured with 120. In Rome, unlike Etruria, gladiatorial combat never had a direct religious significance. But such was the Roman wariness of acting untraditionally that these shows continued to be held under the guise of funerals and mourning. Not that this stopped the shows becoming better staged and more elaborate. The show put on by Titus Flaminius at his father's funeral lasted for three whole days. So did the performance put on in the Forum by Caius Lucan under the slender pretext of honouring a dead paternal uncle.

While Rome was developing its taste for these shows, the real centre of the cult of gladiators lay outside the city in the old strongholds of the Etruscans, particularly to the south of Rome in their former colonies of Lucania and Campania. Here in the provinces the shows were something of a local sport, and a whole organization was evolving to provide for them. This is where the main training centres were. Some of these schools were big – at one time that at Capua had more than two thousand men.

It was at Capua that in 79 BC Spartacus was to start his mutiny of gladiators which at one point threatened Rome itself. And it was in Campania that the *lanistae*, the gladiators' impresarios, built up their *familiae* of fighting men and staged their shows. Here in the provinces some shows would still be theoretically in honour of the memory of a famous man and paid for by his heirs. Others would be donated by elected local magistrates in honour of their town. Still others would be staged straightforwardly for profit and the spectators charged entry. Sometimes the shows were mounted in the open space of the town forum with wooden stands put up for the spectators. More often now, the idea of the old Etruscan fighting pits was being adapted to produce the earliest arenas. The staging was invariably of wood, but by 89 BC the first recorded stone arena had been erected at Pompeii.

Up to this point, Rome had been doing no more than follow external fashions and traditions. Then, quite suddenly, this began to change; during the first century BC the cult of gladiators in Rome was spectacularly transformed. Under the force of changing circumstances it took on its Roman character. As it developed it became an important instrument of power in politics and then in government, until the death-shows and the spectacles surrounding them begin to seem like one of the most ominous experiments in mass government until modern times.

Amphitheatre at Sutri, originally thought to be Etruscan but now accepted as of early Roman origin.

Mosaic of a chariot-race from Lincolnshire, England. British charioteers were introduced into the Roman arena by Julius Caesar after his invasions in 55 and 54 BC.

The first century BC in Rome was a period of anarchy and revolution as the Republic started to collapse under the weight of wealth and military victory. At almost every point, society appeared to have outgrown the institutions of the past. These had evolved for a simpler world – a city-state ruled by its senate and elected magistrates, a settled world of nobles, citizens and slaves, acting and united by their customs and their shared beliefs. The unit was the family; the army was composed of citizens in arms; the world was limited to Rome.

All this was gone or going. Since the defeat of Carthage, Rome had enjoyed a monopoly of power in the Mediterranean. She had become expansionist and cosmopolitan, a world military power. Fortunes had flooded into the city. The emergent Empire was already bursting the seams of the Republic. The population rocketed, morals dissolved, loyalties were shaken, order threatened. Crammed, cosmopolitan Rome was giving the world its first true taste of urban anarchy.

There was no police for a city whose population by the first century BC was approaching half a million. The central government lacked power, generals were fighting generals, demagogues inciting popular unrest, old senatorial families trying to keep position in the mad scramble for office. The 80s saw the Civil War; Rome was shaken by the bitter clash between the democrats and the reaction under Sulla to preserve the Senate's power. Violence counted more and more in politics. Successful military men like Marius and Pompey were now aspiring to total power. Millionaires themselves, they could draw on the resources of other wealthy men. And the traditional ruling class was as corrupt as any; in Rostovtzeff's words it had become 'venal, accepted bribes, and itself bought votes at the elections'.

Pompey, who furthered his political ambitions by using the great spectacles of Rome to enhance his image as popular superman.

There was also a new force within the city – the Roman mob, dependent on the fickle wealth of Rome's new rich, restless and ignorant and waiting to be led. They were the world's first urban proletariat. Against the chaos of their time, they could spell power or confusion for the ambitious leaders fighting for the state. For any one man hoping to rule such a city, the essential problem was not to seize power, but to use it afterwards. There were great fortunes, there was military power, but an effective leader had to have mass support and to impose a modicum of unity on the divisions of the old Republic.

But how? The mass unifying movements of modern history have all relied upon ideas, however simplified or debased – ideas of politics or religion. In Rome this was not possible; religion was too feeble, politics too personal. Power could be seized in certain ways – by rigging the elections to the main elective offices of state, or by straightforward military *coup*. Gracchus had tried the first; Sulla and Crassus, backed by enormous fortunes, tried the second. Marius and Pompey both relied upon the power of their soldiers. Clodius tried to reach power on the shoulders of the mob. All failed, and these aspiring politicians started to learn lessons our modern leaders take for granted. They began attending to their mass appeal. They tried to cultivate the myth of their authority. What they required were images of power which people could appreciate, participate in and obey.

The gradual increase of gladiatorial shows at funerals paid for by rich families makes it clear that people were aware of the power which killing wielded over men's imaginations. The popularity of these bloodthirsty funerals showed, if nothing else, the way that combat to the death could be employed to draw a Roman crowd. Prestige reflected on the donor. It was a form of bribery, and, as a device to please the crowd, the combat proved itself superior to any other form of celebration, such as a banquet or a theatrical performance. Rome's rulers knew this. By the first century people were expecting gladiatorial shows as part of any self-respecting political campaign. In other ways, too, gladiators were becoming a familiar part of Roman life. A troupe of gladiators was a sound investment for a rich capitalist. Outlay and upkeep were expensive, but the returns could be considerable when fighters were hired out for a show. At the same time they seem to have become something of a fashionable hobby for a rich man, just as a string of race-horses might be today. It was quite common for a rich man to maintain a gladiatorial establishment on his estates. The gladiators would rank among the veritable armies of slaves which land-owners were beginning to acquire to work the new vast estates of Italy; and they would also be a useful bodyguard for their master. During the period of the Civil War and the disturbances that followed, gladiators were frequently involved in violence within the city. Clodius employed them to stiffen his gangs of trouble-makers. When Clodius' men clashed with the followers of the wealthy politician, Milo, gladiators fought on both sides.

In ways like these, gladiators had become established as a force in Roman politics by the mid-70s BC. But their full role in Rome's social life and politics first showed itself in the ambitions for supreme power of two men – Pompey and Caesar. Both were great generals. Both were immensely rich, and both tried to build a public cult through which they would be acclaimed popular supermen and rule the state. Pompey tried first. He had won conquests in the East and had enormous military prestige. When he returned to Rome in 62 BC he tried to overawe the city with the impression of his godlike splendour.

Julius Caesar, father of the mass state shows of the Roman Empire.

To do this he staged a triumph of extraordinary magnificence. Nothing was spared. He poured the treasure of the East into his shows, and for the first time cohorts of gladiators were combined with lavish hunts of wild animals, all for the greater glory of one man – Pompey. It didn't work. Pompey had already built up too much distrust among both democrats and senators to get his way. Also, his slaughter of a group of elephants in the arena, which should have been the climax of one of his shows, seems to have backfired. For once the mob was not amused. The destruction of these great docile beasts seems to have roused a sense of pity and disgust even among the Romans. Caesar was cleverer. He could see the political potential of these shows but used them with a certainty of touch which Pompey lacked. He was one of the great impresarios of politics.

In Suetonius' account of Caesar's rise to power it is revealing to see how much attention Caesar devoted to his gladiators. This has been seen by some historians as if it were a sort of gentlemanly diversion, something to take his mind off politics. But Caesar was in far too great a hurry to waste time and money on mere games for their own sake; they were an important part of his campaign to establish his prestige and popular appeal. At a quite early stage in his career, while he was ruthlessly on the make and trying to get himself elected Governor of Egypt by the popular vote, he was already concentrating his resources on public spectacles for the people. He knew his fellow-citizens.

Instead of trying to convince them by his rhetoric, he went all out to entertain them; and this with a lavishness and generosity to show how much he valued them. Certainly he knew exactly how to flatter and excite the masses, how to catch their interest. He held the public office of aedile at the time and used his position to fill the Roman Capitol and Forum with a display of the equipment and material he would be using in his shows. All this was on the grandest scale, and made a great impression. Temporary colonnades were built to stage his hunts and shows.

Some of these he financed himself, others were paid for by his fellow aedile, Marcus Bibulus, who ruefully remarked that either way Caesar would get the credit. One thing that Caesar seems to have understood was the importance of extravagance. He was still borrowing money right and left, but using it on making his shows bigger and grander than any seen within the city. As Plutarch wrote: 'He spent money recklessly, and many people thought he was purchasing a moment's brief fame at enormous price, whereas in reality he was buying the greatest place in the world at inconsiderable expense.'

Other politicians knew what he was up to. For his gladiatorial show, Suetonius reported, he had collected 'so immense a troop of combatants that his terrified political opponents rushed a Bill through the House, limiting the number of gladiators that anyone might keep in Rome; consequently far fewer pairs fought than had been advertised.' Despite this, Caesar's plan worked. Thus, says Suetonius, Caesar secured the good-will of the Commons and their tribunes, and went on to try to become Governor of Egypt. On this occasion Caesar's opponents in the aristocratic party managed to block him, but he had proved the value of his gladiators in a political campaign. Later he tried to set up a big training centre for them in Rome itself. Again his opponents must have understood the power this would give to this ambitious man, and stopped him. But on his victorious return from Gaul, when he was whipping up support for the crucial election to his second consulship, Caesar was once again relying on his gladiators to win the people.

His first move was to announce a massive banquet and gladiatorial show, ostensibly in memory of his daughter Julia. Despite this faint bowing to tradition, Suetonius calls it 'an unprecedented event' – unprecedented because of the hard-headed use Caesar was making of his gladiators. Caesar was immensely practical. Typically, he used every means at his disposal to make this show as grand as possible. He ordered that any well-known gladiator defeated at a show in the circus should not be killed immediately but saved to fight for him. Clearly Caesar understood the importance, not just of numbers, but of the skill of his fighters. Friedländer remarks that 'new gladiators were also trained, not by the usual professionals in the schools, but in private houses by Roman knights and even senators who happened to be masters-at-arms. Letters of his survive, begging these trainers to give their pupils individual instruction in the art of fighting.'

Caesar wanted to make his shows fiercer and more magnificent than before. In the process he became one of the few Romans to add to the Etruscan cult of gladiators. He introduced two new types of gladiator – both of whom incidentally helped enhance his reputation, since both were permanent reminders to Roman audiences of enemies he had fought in his campaigns. One was the Gallic swordsman, dressed in his traditional uniform and fighting in his own style; the other the British charioteer – both were a great success.

In his directness, ruthlessness and flair for crowd psychology, Caesar appears a very modern sort of leader. Through his shows, triumphs, and spectacles, he by-passed the wrangles and the sectional appeals of everyday Roman politics, making a direct, presidential-style appeal to his mass of fellow-citizens. Stendhal once gave his own prescription for seducing a woman: 'If you want to make a bored woman love you, you should conceal the theory, but little by little guide her to an increased activity; you'll soon be a source of pleasure to her.'

This was the principle Caesar was employing to seduce the politically bored Roman populace. Through his great crowds of gladiators he gave them all 'increased activity'. Like Stendhal he soon became a source of pleasure to them all.

It was an incredible performance. For a while Rome became part circus, part arena, with the whole city celebrating the godlike qualities of one man – Caesar. After his final victory over his opponents he held five triumphs to record each of the countries of his victories. In the Gallic triumph he ascended to the Capitol between two lines of forty elephants acting as torch-bearers. In others there were set-pieces on wagons, each tableau representing scenes from his wars. Everyone was benefiting from Caesar's bounty. His legionaries received gratuities in gold and farmsteads to retire to. The Commons who supported him got gifts of grain and oil and gold. Great banquets were held for the people and the shows started, shows such as Rome had never seen before – stage plays, athletic contests, and something new in gladiatorial combats in the

Forum. To flatter the people and show that his appeal could override even the old traditions of nobility, Caesar had paid two noblemen to fight as gladiators – a patrician called Furius Leptinus who fought and killed a former senator called Quintus Calpenus. Young princes from Asia Minor also danced the Pyrrhic sword-dance.

Caesar's wild-beast hunts lasted five days, and were followed by a pitched battle between two armies in the Circus, each army made up of five hundred infantry, twenty elephants and thirty cavalry. Finally he staged a full-scale naval battle between captured Tyrian and Egyptian ships. Apart from casualties among the crews, two senators were included in the members of the watching crowd crushed to death.

All this amounted to an effective transformation of the death-shows as they had developed from the Etruscans. Caesar was concerned with one thing – power – and was prepared to pay whatever price was necessary, either in gold or other people's blood, to keep it. Granted the situation that he faced, it is hard to see what more effective means he could have used to unite his chaotic city round him. He faced a callous and corrupted populace. Other ambitious leaders had already tried subduing it and failed. Caesar succeeded by projecting the impression of his superhuman powers – his lavishness, his strength, his military genius. He did this largely through the medium of shows which he adapted to the needs of the moment.

As impresario Caesar employed the same directness and inventiveness he had shown as a general. He seized on anything that could provide a substitute for genuine political activity. There was the ancient Greek tradition of the athletic games. There was a mock-fight known as the 'Troy Game', supposedly introduced by Aeneas, in which two troops of Roman boys fought one another to show off their military prowess. There was the accepted practice of the military triumph in which the victorious general showed all the trophies of his campaign to the Roman people.

These different elements were merged in Caesar's shows, along with gladiatorial combat and wild-beast hunts. All became a form of propaganda and an important part of Caesar's public cult. Like a good showman Caesar knew exactly how to vary the different themes within these spectacles. They were part rallies, part pageants, part mass pantomimes of power. The Romans were skilled crowd-manipulators. They knew the art of managing the mass excitement of a show, and by the device of the arena Caesar was able now to improvise something of the effect of a successful battle. For the thousands watching one of his carefully staged death-shows there would have been the clash of arms, the splendour of the uniforms, martial music, military skill and the delirium of shedding blood and watching the destruction of an enemy.

The spectators were participating in illusory power. Caesar the showman was permitting them to share in a staged version of his own experience. It was himself he was projecting as the conquering hero, warlike, omnipotent and rich. Rome was a violent city. During the disorders following the Civil War it had seen passions erupting into bloodshed, murder made an acceptable instrument of politics, the city's destiny at risk upon the battlefield. For the Romans violence had become almost an accessory of power. As a realist, Caesar accepted this, and through his shows attempted to confine this public violence. He succeeded, and the tradition of his shows was to prove one of his major legacies to his successors, particularly to his heir, the Emperor Augustus.

The Emperor Augustus greatly enjoyed boxing contests between pugilists such as this one, illustrated on a mosaic from Herculaneum, who is wearing the elaborate thonged gloves of the period.

According to the few descriptions of Augustus that survive, he seems to have had no particular taste for bloodshed. He could be ruthless on occasion, particularly when establishing his position on Caesar's death. After his victory at Perugia, he calmly slaughtered three hundred enemy survivors as an example to all future rebels, and he was always merciless to subsequent threats to his power. But his portrait-busts suggest intelligence and a certain cold superiority of manner which is quite at odds with the distorted features of a monster like Caligula, or a psychotic case like Commodus.

His public life was dedicated to establishing the imperial cult, but in his private life he showed a sensible disdain for grandeur. Augustus lived in an unpretentious house on the Palatine – he wore the clothes woven for him by his wife or daughter, drank little and, whenever possible, ate the coarse food of the ordinary people. In public shows his preferences were for boxing fights rather than for elaborate combats between gladiators – particularly for impromptu bouts between Italians. He had a touch of prudishness too, which caused him to ban women from athletic meetings where males were performing naked. It seems in character that he should have brought the first faint glimmer of humanity to the gladiator's trade by formally banning fights in which defeated gladiators were forbidden quarter. When he heard that Nero's father, Gnaius Domitius, had defied him over this he threatened him with exile.

Yet during the forty-one years of Augustus' reign, Rome's

public shows, including those involving gladiators, steadily increased; not spontaneously either, but as a direct result of the Emperor's personal encouragement. Augustus was entirely involved with them. Once when he was sick he had himself carried to the arena in his litter and presided over the performance lying down. And, unlike Caesar, who had an offhand, condescending air about his public once he had given them a show, Augustus took the fighting seriously. Whereas Caesar used the time at the arena to catch up on his correspondence and even grant an audience or two, Augustus watched the shows from start to finish, and joined the audience in its applause.

Three Vestal Virgins. They had an honoured place in the arena.

Towards the end of his reign he listed his achievements as Emperor. After his victories, his successes and the great buildings he had given Rome, he proudly recorded the ten thousand wild beasts he had provided for the arena and the frequent gladiatorial shows. To quote Suetonius: 'None of Augustus' predecessors had ever provided so many, so different, or such splendid public shows. Gladiators fought, not only in the Circus and the Amphitheatre, but in the Forum and the Enclosure.' Lavish wild-beast hunts and chariot-races were held, and it is noted that he dug an artificial lake beside the Tiber for mock naval battles, the same lake Titus was to use for his nautical games during the inauguration of the Colosseum.

The year 22 BC marks the key point in the development of gladiatorial shows in Rome. This was the year in which, through senatorial decree, Augustus ordered that shows involving gladiators could be held in Rome only by the praetors as part of their official duties. Since praetors were responsible to the Emperor this meant that such shows in Rome at least were effectively an imperial monopoly. If nothing else, Caesar's career had shown how dangerous they could be when they remained in private hands.

Augustus also wanted them for his own purposes. In the first place he appears to have seen them as a means of disciplining Rome and teaching his subjects manners. From the regulations he imposed it seems that he was using the mass shows to create awareness of the new social order of the Empire. This was a direct reversal of how Caesar had behaved. Unlike Caesar, Augustus had no need to discredit the aristocracy. He was no democratic leveller. Quite the reverse. Now that he had the Senate in his hand, it was in his interests to preserve respect for rank. He wanted order. After the years of anarchy Romans had somehow to be trained to respect the Emperor and to keep their places.

Where better could society begin this lesson than in the circus or the amphitheatre, which by their very architecture could be made a living demonstration of a stratified obedient society?

It was put out that the Emperor was outraged when he heard about a senator entering a theatre at Puteoli and not being offered a seat. This was made the occasion for a further senatorial decree ordering that in any public show the front row of the stalls must always be reserved for senators. This was a beginning; further rules followed. Soldiers were separated from civilians, boys from freemen, dark cloaks were forbidden and all women were placed firmly at the back of the house. The sole exception to this last rule was for the vestal virgins who enjoyed pride of place in all state functions.

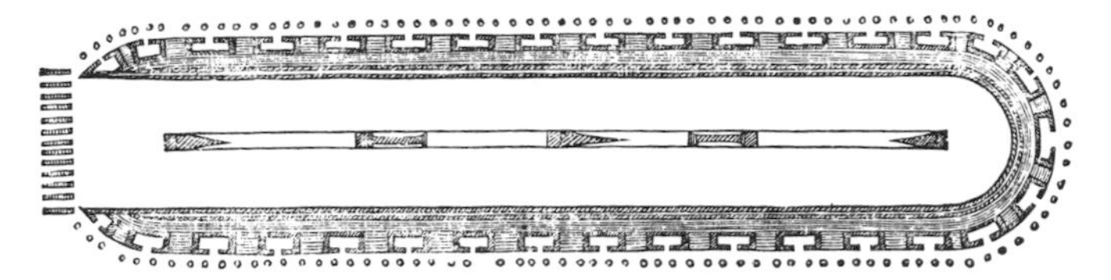

Alberti's reconstruction of the Circus Maximus, from his fifteenth-century treatise on architecture, *De Re Aedificatoria*.

At the same time, Augustus showed that he intended using the spectacles of Rome as an important instrument of government. Much of his energy went into providing appropriate settings for them. His artificial lake, started in 23 BC, was an enormous undertaking, with seats and staging for more than 200,000 spectators. With his direct encouragement the Emperor's friend, Statilius Taurus, built the first stone amphitheatre in the city. And Augustus lavished resources on refurbishing the Circus Maximus. The oldest and the largest of the circuses of Rome, this lay in the long natural declivity below the Palatine. It was an ideal site from which great crowds could watch the games and chariot-races. Caesar had enlarged it, rebuilding chariot stables and having tiers carved from the hillside to accommodate 150,000 spectators. Augustus went still further, making the Circus with its ordered tiers of stone and marble one of the sights of Rome, a clear statement of the order, size and splendour of the Empire. He brought the obelisk of Rameses II from Heliopolis specially to grace the centre of the Circus; over the *cavea*, the rows of seats below the Palatine, he built the *pulvinar*, the special 'royal enclosure' where the Emperor, his family and guests could watch the shows. This was one more development in the imperial cult. From now on this would be the way the Emperor showed himself to his subjects, a godlike creature crowning an immense mass spectacle from the imperial box at the Circus or the arena. As

Carcopino writes, 'the *pulvinar* showed the Romans, overwhelmed by the sight of so much imperial majesty, a sort of first sketch of the future *kathisma* from which the kings would one day command the Hippodrome of Constantinople.'

This coincided with the way the Emperor steadily increased the number of full public holidays in Rome. According to the most reliable estimate, Rome already had 132 days set aside for public games. Most of these days were ancient festivals, but under Caesar a new type of festival appeared – a public holiday decreed by the Senate to commemorate his birthday and five of his most important battles. Once more this proved a precedent Augustus followed. Eighteen new holidays were finally proclaimed in connection with his reign. According to Carcopino's reckoning, there were 153 holidays in the Roman calendar by Augustus' death, of which over 90 were set aside for games given at public expense.

Augustus was effectively transforming the traditional participation of the Roman people in the city's politics. This participation had collapsed with the Republic. No longer had the mass of people any say in government – that was left to the Emperor and his officials. Nor had the ever-rising population of the city any real function in the Empire. Rome was becoming now a static state; the frontiers were settled, the army staffed with foreign professionals, wealth from the provinces and from banking was in the hands of a small group of top wealthy Roman families. But the whole city swarmed with people. Peace and the growing affluence of Rome were carrying the population towards the million mark. Crammed into tenements in the city's slums in Suburra, this proletariat was a standing threat to the magnificence of Rome.

It was to meet this threat that Augustus energetically revived the ancient mass activities of Rome, giving the people a new role in the life of the city. He enhanced their dignity by the great showplaces he built them. He flattered them by his own assiduous presence. From now on the people's role was to provide the audience, the crowd, the extras for the grandiose productions of the Roman Empire.

Caesar had shown the simple truth that mass politics can easily be organized round a vacuum – indeed that it is safer, simpler if they are. The mass politics of the Republic had been concerned with power; the mob was caught up in a naked battle to control the state. The result was anarchy – violence, conspiracies and urban massacre. Caesar avoided this by channelling the emotions of the masses into his shows. Their success had shown that with careful staging public games could form the perfect surrogate for politics.

This use of surrogate politics was a Roman invention which the twentieth century has rediscovered. But we have still to equal the skill and the success with which Augustus used it. He had immense resources to devote to this one purpose, and he constructed the façade of Empire round these great popular events. In the process he developed extraordinary techniques of mass participation in his shows – ritual, religion, mass hysteria. But at the heart of this activity there was nothing, only a game in which the whole audience could forget itself. Or rather several games. Augustus was at liberty to choose from the whole Roman repertoire of races, athletic contests, mock battles, combats to the death. He used them all, but in his reign the greatest spectacle of all was chariot-racing.

Thanks to the size and impressiveness of the Circus Maximus, this was the ideal sport to make the focus of the imperial cult. More than a quarter of a million people at a time could watch the racing. Organized in tiers round the long arena, they could give full rein to that mass emotion which would cause havoc elsewhere in the city. Their instant loyalties could centre on the charioteers; stars like the charioteers Scorpus and Pompeius Musclosus who won over three thousand races were to become the first pop heroes in history. Unlike other heroes, their immense public following was of no danger to the state.

In much the same way, the natural inclination of the people to form groups and factions leading to party conflict under the Republic could be diverted safely to one or other of the teams of charioteers. There were four teams – greens, blues, reds and whites – each with their separate stables, riders, passionate supporters. Rivalry between these different groups came to be every bit as serious as the old rivalries of politics.

But the one vital presence for the people was the Emperor. Throned in the splendour of the *pulvinar*, he was established as the visible embodiment of power. No other ruler until then had built his power in this way. The spectacles of Rome combined the excitement of a major sports event, the disciplined mass will-power of a rally and the emotion of a great religious service. All this reflected on one man – the Emperor. He was above the crowd, above the arguments and petty bickerings of state. His was a superhuman presence, and the claims of his divinity merely gave form to what he was in popular imagination. It was this image of the Emperor as God that began to loom above the great mass spectacles of Rome.

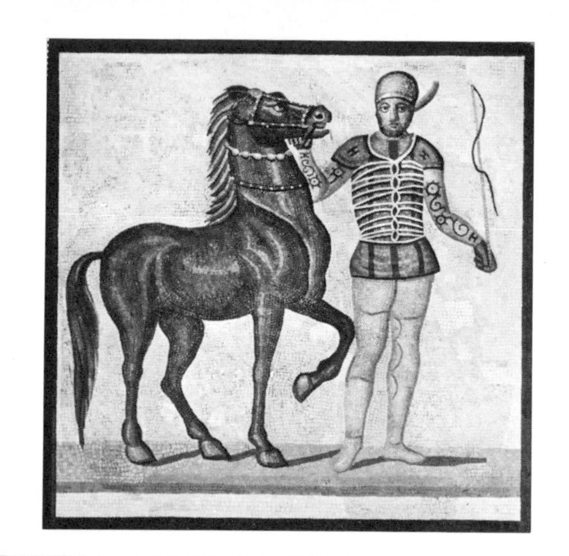

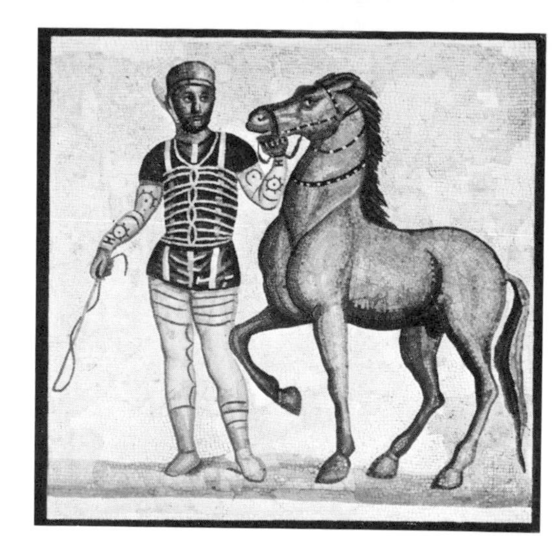

ANNIAE
ARESCVSA

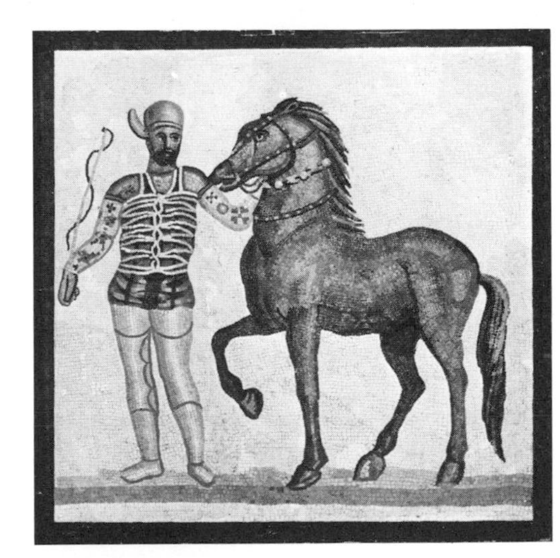

Imperial Rome was chariot-mad. The four mosaics (*above*) show star charioteers with their horses. (*Left*) a charioteer drives his four horses past the winning-post, and (*right*) a triumphant winner carrying the palm of victory.

# III Arena and Disorder

*Myrmillo* depicted on a contemporary Roman lamp.

During the forty-one years of his reign, Augustus made Rome a universal power and a splendid city. Order was maintained, wealth continued to accrue and government was built round the imperial cult. Augustus did this by creating a very modern-seeming form of popular dictatorship whose main expression lay in the Emperor's appearance at the great shows and public spectacles of Rome. Before Augustus' accession these shows were still occasional affairs; great functions such as those put on by Pompey and by Caesar had been made memorable by their rarity. But by the time Augustus died, the mass of Romans were habituated to a continuing round of shows as part of the annual ritual of government.

These great, state-sponsored rallies were something more than a device to conquer boredom in an idle populace. They gave the appearance of a popular foundation to the new Emperor's rule and to the imperial house. They added the prestige of wild and vast enthusiasm to the new régime. Here in these distended ceremonies the might of Rome was suddenly made manifest, the Emperor's power enhanced with all the trappings of a great event.

This mode of government clearly appealed to Augustus. It helped him rule his turbulent city. It gave his Empire a façade of splendour and an emotional appeal. And he was congenitally suited to this sort of rule. Cynical, determined, cold by nature, he was the clever opportunist ready to employ whatever gave him what he wanted. Certainly he had no illusions about human nature; he was quite prepared to exploit the sadism and the mass hysteria of his fellow-Romans. He did this skilfully. He was the greatest of the emperor-impresarios. Through him the shows were organized, controlled to give the maximum political effect.

The official image of the Emperor Augustus. Cameo showing the Emperor enthroned with the allegorical figure of Rome.

But there were dangers in this policy. He was doing what no wise ruler ever does – consolidating power by undermining the emotions and intelligence of his people. Through these great shows, public feeling was becoming trivialized. The aristocracy was being made but one more section of the audience at the arena. Taste was debauched and mass hysteria organized to take the place of genuine expressions of the public will. Worse still, the reality of Rome – its power, traditions, its whole civilizing role – was being systematically replaced in popular imagination by the sadistic fantasies of the arena and the circus. The very splendour of the emperor was becoming simply the apotheosis of a pantomime. With these great shows, vast public buildings and all the trappings of the Empire, the richest power on earth seemed to have mesmerized itself. Static and self-absorbed, Rome was becoming a theatre in which all that mattered was that the show continued.

Under Augustus, all this had one supreme excuse – it worked. Rome was controlled; the emperor was free to rule effectively behind this theatrical façade he had created. After his death the trouble started; the public shows that had been such a source of strength for Caesar and Augustus played a key part in the disasters that afflicted the remainder of their line.

The first hint of trouble came with the accession of Augustus' stepson and successor, Tiberius. Here was a very different character – someone who from the start was clearly torn between his private inclinations and his public role as emperor. He had none of that appetite for power at all costs which had ruled Augustus. One of the few recorded instances of down-to-earth human feeling in the whole history of the Roman emperors came when Augustus ordered Tiberius, as heir-apparent, to reinforce his claims to the throne by marrying his daughter, Julia. Reluctantly Tiberius obeyed, although this meant divorcing Vipsania, the wife he loved. Suetonius has told us that afterwards Tiberius 'continued to regret the divorce so heartily that when, one day, he accidentally caught sight of Vipsania and followed her with tears in his eyes and intense unhappiness written on his face, precautions were taken against his ever meeting her again.'

This glimpse of the unhappy man helps to explain his subsequent behaviour – particularly over the great Roman shows he had inherited from Augustus. Earlier he had seemed to be something of an enthusiast for them, and in the years before accession had personally staged lavish shows in honour of the memory of his father and grandfather, offering star gladiators

The Emperor Tiberius (14–37), a fastidious aristocrat whose hostility to the games made him reviled by all.

a thousand gold pieces each to break their retirement and re-enter his arena. Tiberius was doing his duty by the Empire. These shows were staged at Augustus' suggestion – we know that he even paid for some of them – and were quite clearly a device for helping to proclaim Tiberius as his legitimate undoubted heir. The succession would always be something of a problem in the Empire, and for the heir-apparent to hold his own official shows in Rome would be a useful way for the reigning emperor to establish him in peoples' minds. But even then Tiberius frequently stayed away from the shows held in his honour.

This must have been, like his tears for Vipsania, the true expression of his private feelings about the gladiatorial shows. Much in his make-up would explain his natural dislike for them. He was a fastidious man, an aristocrat with little of Augustus' common touch and none of his willingness to accept the masses for what they were. Greek culture would have made him despise the bloodshed and hysteria of the arena. And as a ruler he conceived his duty to be that of a reformer and a moralist set to restore the ancient qualities of Rome.

He began his reign as a benevolent and civilized reformer using his power to put society to rights. Thanks to Augustus he had reached the throne without dissension; this may have made him over-estimate his powers as he began to fight what was essentially unfightable – the collapsing morals of the city, superstition, promiscuity and the disorders of the Roman mob. For him the passions and mass cruelty of the arena must have appeared anathema – an expression of the disorder and corruption he was facing. Unlike a Caesar or an Augustus, who were quite cynically prepared to build their government on their subjects' weaknesses, Tiberius set himself earnestly and fatally against those weaknesses. He was the only Roman emperor to attempt to rule without the mass state games; all that he proved was that this was just not possible. Courteous, modest, honest as he was, Tiberius was to become a tragic figure whose ideals were broken by political reality.

His stand against the shows was quite determined and consistent from the start. One of his first acts as Emperor was to cut down on the expenses of the public spectacles, lower the pay of actors and set a limit to the number of gladiatorial combats at a given festival. Here his chief motive seems to have been economy. Rome was becoming steadily more show-obsessed and the imperial treasury was obliged to meet a large part of the expense of these extravagances.

But before long Tiberius showed that he had other objections to the arena. As we have seen, Augustus, unlike Caesar, was concerned about the potential danger of the arena to the class structure of the Empire. To prevent the degradation of the senatorial and knightly classes he had banned their members from appearing in the arena. Evidently there had been a loophole to this law. The people so enjoyed watching their betters fight as gladiators that the rewards were high enough to make upper-class wastrels renounce their rank to make their fortunes in the ring. Augustus must have turned a blind eye to such a popular practice. Tiberius would not. From the beginning of his reign, members of the senatorial or equestrian order who had degraded themselves to fight as gladiators found themselves exiled – a law which must have robbed the Roman audiences of some of their star performers.

Soon Tiberius was going further in his reaction against the shows. On grounds of public order he suppressed the traditional city factions whose support of favourite performers sometimes got out of hand and led to bloodshed. Later, at Pollentia in central Italy, some of the local people caused trouble when a centurion died and his heirs refused to stage the usual gladiatorial show in his honour. It was a local upset, nothing more, and in Augustus' day would undoubtedly have been dealt with tactfully from Rome, and Pollentia would have had its show. Tiberius, however, needed an example and was soon treating the affair as a full-scale rebellion. Two companies of troops were sent, citizens arrested, and leading magistrates awarded life imprisonment.

Events like these did little for the Emperor's popularity. His carefulness with money was beginning to be interpreted as meanness; his attempts to restore the strict morality of Rome were usually evaded. Tiberius began to seem an ineffectual prig. Soured by his citizens, this disillusioned idealist soon ran true to form. After the private sorrow at the death of his sons, Drusus and Germanicus, he withdrew entirely from Rome, first to Campania and finally to Capri, where he ended his days abandoned to the worst excesses he had tried to cure in his subjects.

For the administration of the Empire, Tiberius' retreat to Capri was bad enough – the complex mechanism of command started to run down, appointments lapsed, taxes were maladministered, Gaul and Armenia were invaded. But for the Romans, absence was the worst disaster he could have inflicted on them. The city's life was ritualized round the year-long calendar of the Emperor's movements. Temples, theatres and processions, the mass activities of the circus and the arena gave Rome its real identity. The Roman ritual provided the deified Emperor with his essential setting. Overnight it ceased. Without Tiberius Rome was as empty as medieval Rome without its popes. The public show was finished. Rome's million citizens lost their excitement and their way of life.

This sealed Tiberius' unpopularity. The Romans could forgive a reformer or a tyrant emperor but not an absentee. Tiberius did none of the public acts Augustus had performed, provided no great public buildings, offered the citizens no largesse. Most unforgivable of all, the arenas were left empty. For, according to Suetonius, on the rare occasions when he visited the mainland, Tiberius now made a rule against attending any shows. The reason that he gave for this is significant – Tiberius, Suetonius writes, 'gave none himself and did not wish to be asked for any, especially after the crowd forced him, on one of his rare visits to the theatre, to buy the freedom of a slave-comedian called Actius.'

Tiberius, the embittered aristocrat, could not endure the popular invasion of his right to rule by the mob's traditional requests in the arena. At the same time his attitudes to the games can hardly have been sweetened by the news of a disaster at Fidenae in Campania, where an entire amphitheatre collapsed during a gladiatorial show leaving an estimated twenty thousand dead in the wreckage. The catastrophe was great enough to make the Emperor visit it in person, one of the few occasions when he left Capri.

His visit was a gesture, but it did little for his popularity. In old age Tiberius was universally reviled as 'the old goat', miserly and lecherous and cruel. He made one last attempt at a return to Rome but stopped just outside the city by the seventh milestone on the Appian Way. According to one story, this was because of the death of a pet snake, which he found eaten by a swarm of ants. This was interpreted as a warning against the Roman mob. Rather than face them he turned back to Capri, 'the one place where he felt safe', but died on the mainland before he could reach the island. His death was a signal for universal rejoicing, and to show what people felt about his absence from their shows during his reign, the citizens of Misenum tried to persuade the soldiers guarding his funeral cortège to let them burn his body ignominiously in their arena. The guard refused and Tiberius was finally interred in Rome.

Tiberius' reign was something of a lesson for all future emperors. His last years, fearful of the Roman mob, showed the consequence of ignoring the precedent established by Augustus. The new Emperor, Caligula, was determined not to make the same mistake, and he replied to the rejoicing at his accession with a profusion of great shows. This was the most effective way he had of bidding for popularity, and the Romans were delighted, especially when he added a new festival, Parilla, to the calendar of public festivals, and tacked a fifth day on to the Saturnalia, 'to add to the gaiety of Rome'. Work was started on a big amphitheatre beside the Tiber – evidence that Rome was still short of space for full-scale gladiatorial games. For the time being, Caligula had to hold them in the Forum and in the Augustan amphitheatre of Statilius Taurus.

After the first flush of rejoicing, Caligula began to show signs of the strain put on the ruler by the continuous round of popular appearances required by the Roman public. Augustus had been impervious to the curious mirage of power raised by hysterical mass popularity. Caligula was not. He was to be the first of several emperors who were unbalanced by the extraordinary experience of the arena. As his reign progresses one can observe the different stages by which it gradually destroyed him – first the addictive craving for popularity, then the absorption in the unreality of the shows, and finally the relapse into the pathological sadism of the arena's worst excesses.

At the beginning of his reign, Caligula started with the noblest intentions, and for a while it seemed that he would be a conscientious emperor anxious to put right the abuses of Tiberius' last years. Exiles were recalled, judges reinstated, taxes lowered, and he revived Augustus' practice of publishing an imperial budget. Only one thing appeared to mar his future – his obsessional desire to be liked. It was important to maintain good relations with the Roman mob – Augustus had done this – but Caligula was willing to do anything for applause. Certainly Augustus would never have permitted magistrates in Rome to preside at an official gladiatorial show in place of the Emperor, nor would he have seen the need for the celebrations Caligula now introduced in a fresh bid for popularity. These affairs had little of the purposeful state ritual of Augustus' shows. Here there was no restraint as Caligula started buying people's gratitude. Vouchers were scattered at performances to give the audience a basket of food apiece. Rome was illuminated by night, and all-day shows mounted in the Circus, where once more the people had the thrill of watching senators driving the chariots. Caligula personally introduced a new turn in the ring – panther-baiting – and on one occasion when he was visiting the arena to inspect some new equipment some bystanders called out – 'How's about a day's racing, Caesar?' This appealed to him and without another thought he gave orders for a show to start.

Increasingly his life centred on the arena. This was an obsession now, and it was clear that the hysteria and sadism of the shows was starting to affect him. Instead of using the excitement of the arena, as Augustus had, to lead up to the audience's submission to his divine self, Caligula began to see in it a chance to act out sadistic fantasies in public. Augustus had used the shows to rule – Caligula to commit atrocities.

At first he seemed content with any titillation he could get from organizing special shows. When he felt bored with the published show, he would enliven the proceedings by ordering old gladiators to fight decrepit criminals. Their feeble duels to the death amused him. So did another of his specialities – making deformed men fight as gladiators. He is said to have been put out by the cost of butchers' meat for the arena animals and to have fed them condemned criminals on grounds of economy, supervising the choice of human meat in person.

The depravity of Caligula revealed itself in the arena, but did not stop there. Soon it was finding victims beyond the gladiators and criminals. One of the first was the man who managed his gladiatorial shows for him. He upset the Emperor and, with an excessive show of poetic justice, Caligula watched him being flogged with chains for several days, having him killed 'only when the smell of suppurating brains became intolerable'. After the manager it was a playwright's turn – he was burned to death in the arena because of a *double entendre* in a play which upset Caligula. Finally the audience, too, had to suffer. From his all-powerful position on the podium, Caligula had realized how vulnerable they were. He enjoyed watching scuffles which he provoked by having gift vouchers left on the seats reserved for knights, thus causing common people to invade their rows. He also liked observing the discomfort of the audience when at the hottest time of day he had the canopies drawn back from the arena and all the doors bolted.

Finally, Caligula's cruelty overflowed; all Rome became his arena and the terror started. Citizens were arbitrarily arrested, tortured, put to death. Men of good family might be branded for no reason, thrown to the beasts, and even, according to one account, sawn in half. There seemed no reason for these

The Emperor Caligula (37–41), whose depravity revealed and expressed itself in the arena.

persecutions except the Emperor's madness. Possibly the key to them lies in the fact that they all formed sadistic spectacles in themselves. Caligula's favourite mode of execution came to be through small wounds that avoided vital organs so as to make the victim 'feel that he is dying'. He is said to have enlivened his banquets by having people tortured while his guests were eating, and his most memorable murder well might have been an incident from some spectacular public show. He had a bridge of boats built across the bay at Puteoli. When it was complete and crammed with people he produced a great disaster by having them all tipped suddenly into the sea.

Disasters seem to have obsessed him – a further symptom of the sadistic delusions of omnipotence the arena roused in him. Caligula was heard lamenting that there were no more genuine disasters, equalling the collapse of the amphitheatre at Fidenae, and often prayed for military catastrophe, for fire or plague or earthquakes. It was as if the morbid fascination of the Roman mob at the arena had finally produced this monster to chastise them. For, like his uncle, the Emperor Tiberius, Caligula too had come to hate this people he once tried to charm. 'I wish all you Romans had but one neck,' he shouted at the great audience at his games. The cruelty of the arena had come full circle and was threatening the spectators.

During the last stages of the Emperor's madness the arena was the setting for his nightmares. This produced the final parody of the solemn ritual of the Emperor-God, as Caligula entered the arena to fight his gladiators in duels with wooden swords. To please the Emperor, one of the combatants fell down beneath his blows. Caligula drew a dagger, stabbed him to death, and ran round the arena with the palm of victory.

Soon he was becoming jealous of the fame of star performers. Whereas Augustus realized that the brief popularity of a successful gladiator offered no threat to the Emperor of Rome, Caligula interpreted popular success as a personal affront. He was even envious of the good looks of a centurion's son called Aesius Proculus, and had him dragged without warning from his seat in the amphitheatre and matched against a Thracian net-fighter and a man-at-arms. When the young man won both fights this must have doubled the offence; Caligula had him chained and dressed in rags and dragged through the streets to execution. Later a chariot-fighter called Parius earned such applause that Caligula stormed out of the stadium. In doing this he tripped over his robe, fell down the steps, and complained furiously that the most powerful race in the world paid more heed to a gladiator's trifling gesture than to all their deified emperors. The Emperor's degradation was complete. He had caught the arena madness as badly as the meanest citizen. The unrealities of this dream-world meant more to him than his position as the most powerful man on earth.

When his death came it took a form appropriate for such an emperor; the arena which had played such a part in his madness now formed the setting for his murder. He was stabbed during an interval at one of his shows while talking to some Trojan dancers. Yet even now his popularity persisted. Despite his madness and appalling cruelties he was, according to Josephus, 'honoured and loved by the folly of the populace. . . . The distributions of food, the games and the gladiatorial combats had won their hearts, for such were the delights of the mob.'

Indeed, with several emperors now, there is a sense that all that really matters is their role as actors, as they are borne along in the continual show in which they are the one indispensable star. When Claudius succeeded his lamented nephew, he continued to employ the public shows to set the style of his government and ensure his popularity. All that had changed was the emperor's personality. Caligula had played the psychopath before the mob. Claudius acted the buffoon.

'At public games he would rise with the audience and show his delight by clapping and shouting. When the tribunes of the people appeared before his judge's chair, he apologized for not offering them a seat. This sort of behaviour endeared him to the people from the start.' Claudius wanted to be everybody's friend and offered Rome a shower of games, attempting to unite the city in popular rejoicing. The Guards were even given their own private shows in camp, 'without wild beasts or fancy equipment'. The citizens were offered gladiatorial games in the Forum and the Enclosures, and Claudius devised a new show, very much his own. As it was popular he frequently repeated it. He called it his 'Picnic', and through heralds invited everyone to come to the arena and 'take pot-luck, as it were'.

In contrast with the cumbrous ritual of Augustus, the key-note of these 'Picnics' was their informality, the Emperor acting as the easy-going friend of the people, personally counting out the prize-money as he awarded it, calling the audience 'My Lords' and cracking what Suetonius called 'stupid and far-fetched jokes' with the people. When they yelled, 'Bring on the Dove' – the Dove being the nickname of a famous gladiator – Claudius shouted back: 'Sure, but he'll take a bit of catching.'

Pretending to identify himself with the people, Claudius enjoyed the chance to make the sort of sentimental gesture that had so annoyed the aristocratic Tiberius. On one occasion four brothers pleaded before Claudius in the arena for the freedom of their father, a successful chariot-fighter. He must have been an outstanding gladiator to have survived so long and it suited Claudius to give the people what they wanted; amid resounding cheers he gave the man the wooden sword, the gladiator's symbol of honourable retirement. But Claudius was also shrewd enough to use the moment to point an important moral for the state. When the cheers subsided he had the herald say: 'You now see the advantage of having a large family; it can win favour and protection, even for a gladiator.'

Indeed, unlike his two predecessors, Claudius seemed to understand the propaganda value of the shows, and sometimes used them to project a public image of himself as the heroic servant of the state. There was an echo of Julius Caesar's staging of his Gaulish battles in the Circus Maximus in the show that Claudius put on in the Campus Martius. To remind the Romans of his British exploits, his gladiators acted out the storm and sacking of a foreign town, after which Claudius appeared in his purple campaign cloak presiding at a tableau of the British king's surrender.

This was a very different Claudius from the genial provider of the 'Picnics'. But Claudius lacked the style to sustain these flights of grandeur; the touch of the ridiculous which went down well at his informal shows marred the effect of his full-scale productions. For all the trouble that he took, the show he planned to celebrate the completion of the canal from the Fucine Lake made Claudius the laughing-stock of Rome.

Again, he modelled this performance on the productions of the great age of the massed imperial shows – this time on the sea-fight which Augustus had staged in his *naumachia* beside the Tiber. The theme was the ancient battle between Rhodes and Sicily. Twelve full-sized triremes, manned with gladiators, were drawn up on each side. A mechanical Triton, made of silver, would rise from the bottom of the lake and sound the attack by blowing on a conch. (No one has explained how this machine worked, but Rome's shows provided an important outlet for Roman technology in a pre-industrial world.)

At the last minute, Claudius nearly created a fiasco. When his gladiators gave him the traditional greeting – 'Hail, Caesar, we salute you, we who are about to die,' – he replied flippantly, 'or not, as the case may be'.

The imperial buffoon. The Emperor Claudius as Jupiter.

(*Left*) the *coup de grâce.*

(*Right*) *paegniarii*, mock-fighters, acted as curtain-raisers before the killing started. They used no weapons, only sticks and whips.

It was not quite the moment for cheap humour. Neither Caesar nor Augustus would have committed such a solecism, for gladiators, like all performers, had to be taken seriously. The result of Claudius' joke was one of the few occasions when Roman gladiators refused to fight. Deeply offended, they insisted that Claudius' remark amounted to a pardon. After this they sulked. This soon revealed the hollowness of Claudius' good nature, and what followed was most Italian. Claudius, feeling his *figura* threatened, flew into a rage and threatened to send in troops to set their ships alight. This had no effect. The gladiators stayed on strike, and Claudius must have realized that a massacre would spoil the day's festivities. So he calmed down sufficiently to hobble to the lakeside and urge them not to disappoint their public. This evidently restored their self-respect; the fighting started.

The arena usually revealed the character of the emperors – even in the case of Claudius. While no Caligula, he showed that, for all his assumed good nature, he enjoyed bloodshed. He was the emperor who made the cruel law that any gladiator who accidentally slipped should automatically have his throat cut.

*Retiarius*, as he appears on a medallion from a pottery vase.

According to one writer, this was done because Claudius enjoyed watching gladiators die, and he was particularly anxious to have the rule enforced against the *retiarii*. Since they wore no helmets he could observe their death agonies on their faces. Claudius' morbid interest in the arena often kept him there from daybreak to the lunchtime interval. Even this was sometimes not enough, and he would dismiss the audience and sit alone in the amphitheatre, ordering the gladiators to continue fighting. When they had had enough he even ordered stage-hands into the ring to fight.

After the murder of Claudius and the accession of his adopted son, Nero, there was a repetition of the lavish public shows which had become the accepted way of welcoming a new reign. Since Augustus first used the shows to establish young Tiberius as his heir, these accession games had turned into something like a coronation ceremony for the new emperor. By holding them, he was demonstrating his right to rule. By attending them, the people were adding their tacit affirmation of the fact. Nero's games celebrated this in a mammoth act of official rejoicing and extravagance.

From the beginning Nero was show-mad and, unlike Caligula, something of an expert at the games. As a boy he had become a skilful charioteer, taking the sport so seriously that he regularly consumed the charioteers' specific against damage in a fall – ashes of boar-shit mixed with water. He also thrilled the audience at the Circus by racing a chariot harnessed with four camels. From such an emperor the Roman mob expected something special in his inaugural games. They were not disappointed. Nero adored his public role and proceeded to outdo himself in a production which he entitled 'The Great Festival'.

Here was something different from the extravaganzas staged by Caligula and Claudius at their accession. As well as being a dedicated charioteer, Nero was also something of an artist and a poet, a cultivated youth who saw himself as the exemplar of Hellenistic culture, and the Great Festival reflected this. The centre of the Festival took the form of various elaborate plays and pageants devoted to the theme of his perpetual reign. But each performance was ingeniously expanded into something of a mass event which every Roman would appreciate. The play was used as an excuse for music, dancing, circus turns which were included in the action, and Nero showed great skill in gaining the attention of the massive audience. He persuaded aristocrats and well-known social figures to take parts in the play. In one of them a Roman knight is said to have ridden an elephant down a sloping tightrope, and during a production of Afranius' play *The Fire* a complete house was actually set alight on stage. As an additional excitement, there was the sight of the whole cast scrambling to rescue valuable possessions from the blaze. The house was richly furnished and Nero had announced that they could keep whatever they could save.

Not only the actors benefited. 'Throughout the Festival all kinds of gifts were scattered to the people – one thousand assorted birds daily and quantities of food parcels; besides vouchers for corn, clothes, gold, silver, precious stones, pearls, paintings, slaves, transport animals and even trained wild beasts – and finally for ships, blocks of city tenements and farms.'

The Emperor Nero (54–68). Show-mad since boyhood, he was an excellent charioteer and his 'Great Festival' was the supreme spectacle of his day.

The Empire and its Emperor were immensely rich, and Nero was employing the public shows to create a tableau of the whole of Rome sharing the good fortune of the times. It was a strange conception, a mammoth exercise in mass theatricals. For all its wealth, Rome was a cruel city, horribly overcrowded, insanitary, dangerous, unjust. For the majority of Romans life

was obscenely harsh. Crammed in the slums of Suburra, they lived precariously beneath the grandiose symbols of the Empire, a hopeless mob surviving in the midst of ostentatious luxury. These were the Romans that Tiberius ignored, and came to fear. And these were the Romans Nero was including in his shows. It was impossible to change their world, so they were being offered dreams, the dream of finding themselves made rich, or of participating in occasions of luxury and vast extravagance.

Most of the mass emotions behind Nero's shows find an echo in the appeal of modern television, where even greater audiences identify with the participants in give-away shows, join in the dangerous thrills of car- and speedway-racing, and get vicarious enjoyment from the lives of the glamorous and rich. Nero achieved the same effects in the first century AD through an extraordinary exercise in mass entertainment. Thanks to his imagination and extravagance, Rome had a chance to live a waking dream. Nero himself, this dedicated showman-emperor, was starting to enjoy the illusion of power freed from all human limitations. In his arenas and circuses, in this showpiece of a city, he could make reality what he pleased.

Caligula had discovered this when he inflicted his morbid fantasies on to the arena. Nero was acting more benevolently – and more ambitiously. In his Great Festival he was attempting to create theatrical illusion on a superhuman scale. To do this properly he required more arena space than Rome possessed. The big arena started by Caligula beside the Tiber had not been finished. Clearly it had been conceived on too great a scale for the resources of the Empire at the time; only a determined government with full control of its resources could hope to carry through a massive public work on such a scale. Nero was not the man to do it, either. He was impulsive and extravagant. Theatre-lover that he was, he required instant effects and regarded architecture as a branch of scenery. So he abandoned Caligula's barely started stone arena and had an amphitheatre built of wood on a site in the Campus Martius. This took his workmen less than a year to finish and it was here that he offered Rome the gladiatorial games that were expected of him.

In one essential Nero's inaugural games must have disappointed the Roman crowd. The gladiators were not allowed to kill. This ban of Nero's has never been explained. Perhaps it is significant that Nero's former tutor, Seneca, was almost the one educated Roman at this time to have written against the inhumanity of the slaughter. Certainly, as an artist and a dedicated lover of the Greek theatre, Nero would have seen the mass delight in gladiators' deaths as something tasteless and uncivilized.

Instead he tried to turn the fights into occasions of unrivalled splendour. In one show all his gladiators had accoutrements of amber, and, once again, he tried to overwhelm the audience by the extravagance, the pageantry and the theatrical illusions at his command. The poet Calpurnius described how the ground was made to open, so that a magic wood of glittering bushes and fountains sprang to view, inhabited by foreign monsters snarling from the earth. The animals were killed. Nero had no objection to killing animals; indeed on one occasion he had a mounted squadron of the Praetorian Guard take on four hundred bears and three hundred lions in the arena. But his real interest seems to have been in creating illusions – magic fountains, floating palaces, a lake that filled with sea-water teeming with rare monsters from the furthest oceans. Sometimes these conjuring tricks of his were cheerfully obscene. During a tableau based upon the Minotaur an actor dressed up as a bull mounted a hollow wooden heifer. And sometimes there were accidents; an actor playing Icarus fell during flight and landed near the Emperor, spattering him with blood.

The philosopher Seneca, Nero's tutor and one of the very few Romans whose conscience was pricked by the arena.

During Nero's reign the staging of the shows seems to have reached unheard-of heights of ingenuity, but in the process they were becoming less and less what they had been under Augustus – solemn affairs of state and part of the ritual of government. Increasingly, they reflected little beyond this stage-struck youth's theatrical obsession. As if to emphasize the way the shows were changing character, he now refused to show himself to his people at the performances in the arena. Instead, like a modern stage director, Nero kept out of sight. The show, not the Emperor, was what mattered, and Nero preferred to watch the spectacle through a window in the closed imperial box.

Like Caligula, Nero must ultimately be counted among the victims of Rome's public shows. It was a strange fate. Just as the eighteenth-century monarchy in France became so fatally cut off from all reality within its dream-world of Versailles, so Nero lost himself to the illusory world he could create in Rome. Little else mattered when compared with the limitless possibilities the shows could offer such a man. Why bother with the cares of Empire when he could accomplish anything he wished within this great theatre of a city? What mattered if the treasury were empty or his government neglected? The shows were more important, for they kept the mob in order and the

Nero in his favourite role, of Apollo the divine musician.

Emperor happy. And just as with Caligula, this dream-world gradually unbalanced Nero's unsteady mental equilibrium.

His degeneration followed much the same course as Caligula's. Nero was more cultured, more intelligent, but the corruption of the arena and the shows was to produce in him much the same effect, the same divorce from all reality, neglect of government and envious involvement with the popular figures of the arena. Caligula gave Eutychus the charioteer over two million sesterces and made him for a while the most influential man in Rome. Nero gave Spicullus the gladiator 100,000 sesterces for a single show and made Tigellinus, the charioteer and horse-breeder from Calabria, his wealthiest favourite.

Soon, as in Caligula's case, Nero was not content with merely putting on the shows. He needed to participate as well. His earlier successes as a charioteer were not enough. After his trip to Greece he needed to be acclaimed the greatest artist in the world. Even this dream was possible. Caligula had been dutifully applauded by the mob for his grotesque combats as a gladiator. Nero was similarly applauded for his efforts as a poet and a singer. His great ambition was for immortality, not as emperor, but as a singer and an athlete and a charioteer. Despite the weakness of his voice – he used enemas and emetics in the belief that they would strengthen it – he gave a two-day concert to a vast audience at Naples, where the applause was led by a claque, five thousand strong, organized on his behalf by a group of knights. In Rome he took the parts of gods and heroes in public shows, again to vast applause, and was delighted to be compared with the god, Phoebus Apollo, for his singing and his chariot-driving. According to one story, he also longed to be remembered as a Hercules, and so he had a lion carefully trained so that he could face it in the arena and kill it with his hands or with a club. Just as Caligula had been so envious of the mob's enthusiasm for Parius, the chariot-fighter, so Nero was rumoured to have arranged the death of Paris, the actor, believing him to be a dangerous rival.

And the arena finally brought out that vein of cruelty in Nero for which he is remembered. Again it is significant that, as with other emperors, his most memorable atrocities took the form of circus acts. Even the Emperor's sadism was theatrical. There were the Christian martyrs covered in pitch and used to illuminate his gardens as human torches; and he devised a form of execution which in its exquisite refinement remains unique. This was the *tunica molesta*, a splendid robe, embroidered with gold and glittering with precious stones, which a condemned criminal was forced to wear in the arena. The robe was specially prepared so that at the climax of the show it burst into flames.

As his disorder spread, even his private life appeared as a continual melodrama, totally divorced from all reality. He was the central actor in his own theatre of the absurd. He could change any relationship at will, just as a theatrical director changes the characters his actors have to play. What was to stop him turning his current favourite, Sporus, into a woman by having him castrated, and then marrying him? Equally, what was to prevent his freedman, Doryphorus, marrying Nero in his turn? On this wedding night Nero is said to have played the part of a young girl with gusto, imitating the moans of a virgin being deflowered.

With such a character, anything could be believed, for anything was possible – incest and even matricide. When he felt he needed fresh excitement he was reputed to have roamed the streets at night with gladiators, beating up citizens and breaking into houses. It was another role for him to play.

Even the final act of Nero's life – the predictable retreat into a private world – was done theatrically. He was no Tiberius to flee the Roman mob and find his peace and pleasure in Capri.

He had to build his private world in Rome itself, and seemed unable to conceive of it except in terms of the illusory world of the arena. This was his fabled 'Golden House'. When it was finished Nero exclaimed: 'Now I can live as a human being should.'

This Roman Xanadu will always be an architectural conundrum. All that remains today are some of the foundations and several enigmatic, melancholy cellars. But from contemporary accounts it seems that this was a miniature Versailles built in the heart of Rome. Nero took more than five hundred acres of the crowded city centre, turning them into parkland and a big ornamental lake, in Suetonius' words, 'more like a sea than a lake, surrounded by buildings made to resemble cities, and by a landscape garden consisting of ploughed fields, vineyards, pastures and woodlands, where every variety of domestic and wild animal could roam at will'.

It was scene-setting on the grandest scale, an attempt to re-create those magic woodlands and theatrical effects Calpurnius described in the arena. But it was the actual palace that was the wonder of its day. A colossal statue of the Emperor, 120 feet high, stood in the entrance hall. Parts of the house were overlaid with gold and set with mother-of-pearl and precious stones. 'All the dining-rooms had ceilings of fretted ivory, the

panels of which could slide back and let a rain of flowers, or of perfume from hidden sprinklers, shower upon the guests. The main dining-room was circular, and its roof revolved slowly, night and day, in time with the sky. Sea-water or sulphur-water was always on tap in the baths.'

Reading this early account of Nero's Golden House one understands how totally he had become the victim of his public role. This was no real house – it was a theatre. Even when he attempted to escape and find some solitude where he could 'live as a human being should', he had to re-create the mirror world of the proscenium and the arena. The wonders of the place were clearly the invention of those masters of illusion, Rome's theatrical engineers, whose incredible effects were already turning the arena into a wonderland. At this crisis of his life, all that this Emperor could do was to retreat into yet more illusion, building himself a private stage where he could continually perform.

Building the Golden House was an anti-social act and quite contrary to the policy established by Augustus. Augustus had lived simply, but had built extravagantly for Rome. Nero was building for himself alone, and in the process taking much-needed land from the crowded city after the great fire of Rome –

an act that undoubtedly increased his unpopularity. But the key fact that sealed his fate before the revolt by the future Emperor, Galba, was his withdrawal into his private fantasies. Had he been able to consolidate his popularity in Rome, as he had done at the beginning of his reign by uniting the people in the great spectacles, he could have been impregnable. Instead he acted out his doom like the demented victim of a running melodrama, posturing, quoting, weeping like the ham-actor that he was. During his last days his fantasies as a performer seem to have blotted out reality and prevented him from taking any effective measures against his enemies. As Galba advanced, the Emperor composed songs against him. As he got closer, Nero sent a message to an actor warning him not to push himself forward during the Emperor's absence from the stage on affairs of state. When he was assembling his army, Nero's chief concern was to find wagons for his stage equipment. Even his death appeared symbolic of the disasters the arena had brought to Rome and its emperors. Lacking the courage to kill himself, Nero called on his gladiator, Spiculus, to do the deed. But Spiculus had left him and Nero, the last of the line of the Caesars, managed to stab himself. Through his last tears he spoke his own typically overblown obituary: 'Dead! And so great an artist.'

(*Left*) reconstruction of the wall decoration of Nero's Golden House.

(*Above*) the scale and splendour of the Golden House must have been similar to this Roman villa, depicted on a fresco from Pompeii.

# IV Vespasian

The Emperor Galba, who first gained the attention of the Roman people by having elephants walk a tight-rope in the arena.

Upon Nero's death, Rome's year of anarchy began and AD 69 went down in history as the memorable 'Year of the Four Emperors', three of whom met violent deaths. This was the year in which the Roman Empire seemed to have become one vast arena in which successive emperors battled for power, cheered on by the populace of Rome. The decisive power lay with the army. There were no real Roman politics by now. Augustus' policy of substituting mass games for mass political activity had reached its inevitable conclusion. The aristocracy were played out; Rome seemed devoid of aims, beliefs, or popular opinion above the level of the circus and the arena. During the catastrophes of this year the only part the Roman people played was that of an audience, watching the rival generals and quite willing to accept whoever could seize power and make the show continue. Tacitus was later to complain of the people's 'brutish indifference' to their emperors' fate. 'As if this were one more entertainment in the festive season, they gloated over horrors and they profited by them, careless which side won and glorying in the calamities of the state.'

Tacitus was not exaggerating, and it is extraordinary how much this period of anarchy seemed to be dominated by the arena and the public shows. Nero's successor, Galba, had first made his name when, as praetor in charge of the Floral Games, he gave the Roman people the novel spectacle of a troop of tightrope-walking elephants. This was remembered by the people when, as successful general and ex-Governor of Spain and Africa, he led the military *coup* that ended Nero's reign. Not that the memory of his elephants served any purpose when Galba's discontented troops disposed of him in his turn and placed the ineffectual Otho on the throne. But with the next

Vespasian, the shrewd peasant emperor. His reign restored sanity to the Empire.

Vitellius, the imperial glutton, whose rise to fame and power, like that of so many emperors, depended on the arena.

candidate for power, the gross Vitellius, it was as if the Roman games were suddenly putting forward their own man as emperor. This greedy sycophantic courtier had made his career by pandering to successive emperors' obsessions with the games. He won Caligula's favour by his skill as a circus charioteer and often ran the shows at which Nero sang or recited his poetry – a supreme test for any time-server. Rumour said that he received the governorship of Lower Germany thanks to the influence of a fellow-supporter of the 'Blues' in the Circus, and his immediate reaction to Otho's suicide was to stage celebratory all-night games for his supporters. As emperor, Vitellius appointed as his chief adviser Asiaticus, his catamite and freedman and a former gladiator.

Vitellius' accession and his death were both occasions for the mob to show their fickleness and cruelty. As his troops moved on Rome the people had stormed the imperial palace yelling for Otho's death, 'just as they would have called for a fresh turn in the arena'. But when Vitellius' brief and unelevating reign was over, the people, in Tacitus' phrase, 'dishonoured his death with the same base passion that they honoured his life'. Enthusiastically they turned to welcome the next contender in this battle of the emperors. Sixty years old, a successful general and a widower with two grown sons, Vespasian had made his reputation in the Jewish War. He was a self-made man, of peasant stock from Sabine country to the north of Rome. Somewhat uncouth, devoid of any of the courtly graces, he seemed the sort of man the people understood. His popularity increased when he announced one of the first decisions of his reign, that the land taken up by Nero's Golden House would be returned to the Roman people. The ornamental lake beyond the Forum would become the site of a great amphitheatre to be named after the Emperor's family.

Vespasian was to be one of the great surprises of the Empire. At this low point of anarchy and degradation, Rome had discovered its salvation in this unlikely old outsider who seemed to have stumbled on the throne by chance. People were impressed by his solidity and common sense, and like the shrewd Sabine peasant that he was he calmly set about dealing with the crisis. He was no innovator. His chief concern was with restoring confidence and order to the city, and building the imperial finances after the insane extravagances of Nero and Caligula. Apart from common sense, Vespasian possessed one quality which made him virtually unique among the Roman emperors – a sense of humour. He never took himself too seriously. Suetonius quotes him saying, when caught in the slow crawl of his triumph: 'What an old fool I was to demand a triumph, as though I owed this honour to my ancestors or ever made it one of my ambitions. It serves me right.' His words on his death-bed, too, were to become something of a classic of their kind. 'Dear me,' the deified old Emperor said, when he realized he was past recovery, 'I must be turning into a god.'

The other facts recorded of Vespasian's character seem to accord with the few portrait-busts of him that survive. This is no cold, withdrawn leader like Augustus or Julius Caesar, nor an embittered aristocrat like Tiberius. This is a clever practical face and very tough. His father was a tax-gatherer turned banker, one of the new men who had been quick to take advantage of the financial opportunities of the Empire. Vespasian too had been a considerable opportunist. He had survived the enmity of Nero – caused, according to one story, when he fell asleep at one of the Emperor's recitals – and for a while endured great poverty. As a general he had been obstinate, methodical and realistic. He showed the same qualities as emperor.

His wide experience and age must have helped prevent the hot-house atmosphere of court from turning his head, as it had with all his predecessors since Augustus, and it was totally in character for him to continue living his private life quite simply with an aging mistress. He was pre-eminently, somewhat tediously, sane. He was also the least vindictive of men, giving Vitellius' daughter a dowry, and reputedly becoming upset at the execution of criminals. Even his dominating vice, his meanness, must have appeared as something of a virtue in a Roman emperor.

Unlike a Nero or a Vitellius, this tax-collector's son knew the power of money – and how to raise it. He is remembered as the Emperor who taxed the latrines of Rome. When his son, Titus, said this was unworthy of him, Vespasian handed him a coin, the first-fruit of the new tax, and asked him, 'Does it smell, my son?'

Vespasian must seem the last man likely to have made grandiose, expensive gestures for the fun of it, which makes it all the harder to explain why he embarked on such an undertaking as the Colosseum. One thing is certain; he would not have started such a project unless he thought it absolutely necessary. The reasons for it lay at the very centre of his policy.

From the beginning of his reign, Vespasian was the great rebuilder, 'the second Augustus', working to the first Emperor's blueprint. He seems to have had a very clear idea of what he wanted. He was no idealist like Tiberius, still less did he share nostalgic dreams for the Golden Age of the Republic. Nero's closed Oriental despotism was obnoxious to him, too.

His main concern was to realize the vast potential of the Empire and to make the centralized administration work after the chaos left behind by Nero. This was to be his great achievement. He restored the battered frame of government and Rome revived as the trading and financial centre of the world. With this revival went an upsurge of the Emperor's fortune – Vespasian saw to that – and like Augustus he used the great imperial resources to make Rome once again the visible expression of the greatness of the Empire.

Vespasian was an obsessive builder. Much of Rome needed reconstructing after the fire during Nero's reign. Vespasian authorized anyone who pleased to take over the sites of ruined houses and to start building if no owners claimed them. He personally began the work of restoring the burned Capitol by carrying the first basketful of rubble on his shoulders. But as well as restoration he started two new temples – one to Peace, near the Forum, and one to the deified emperor, Claudius (all these in addition to the Colosseum). Building on this scale served a propaganda purpose. These overwhelming structures offered visible proof of the wealth, stability and power of the emperor. Under the universal peace of the Empire there was no longer any opportunity for an emperor to impress the population at first hand with military prowess. Vespasian, like Augustus, chose to express his power in feats of building rather than feats of arms. And just as the Emperor was ascribed divinity, so his great buildings were conceived on a godlike scale. Nobody but the Emperor-God could build like this. The individual could only feel his insignificance against such massiveness. The very scale of the Colosseum was an assertion of Vespasian's attempt to make the Empire fulfil Augustus' intentions and endure.

On a more immediate level, Vespasian's decision to commence the great amphitheatre was a bold gesture every Roman must have understood. He was attempting what three emperors had already tried to do. Augustus, Caligula and Nero had all thought of such a building. Augustus planned it but never started; Caligula started but got little further; Nero settled for an amphitheatre built of wood. Vespasian was attempting a great *tour de force* which would inevitably impress Rome with the power of his name and of his ruling house. It would be a living monument of the benevolence the Emperor felt towards the Roman people. This was his gift to them, something for which the most ungrateful member of the mob might feel some gratitude, and a reminder that Vespasian was giving back to Rome the land that Nero stole to build his Golden House.

At the same time, by starting the Colosseum, Vespasian was also showing that, just like Augustus, he intended to continue the great mass spectacles as part of the ordered ritual of the Empire. Above all else, his amphitheatre demonstrated a clear-cut and decisive understanding of the relationship between spectators, combatants and emperor. It was planned so precisely and on such a scale that it laid down the role that each ideally should play in the perpetuating drama of the Roman Empire.

Reconstruction of the Colosseum made by Carlo Fontana in his book *L'Anfiteatro Flavio descritto e delineato*, published in 1725.

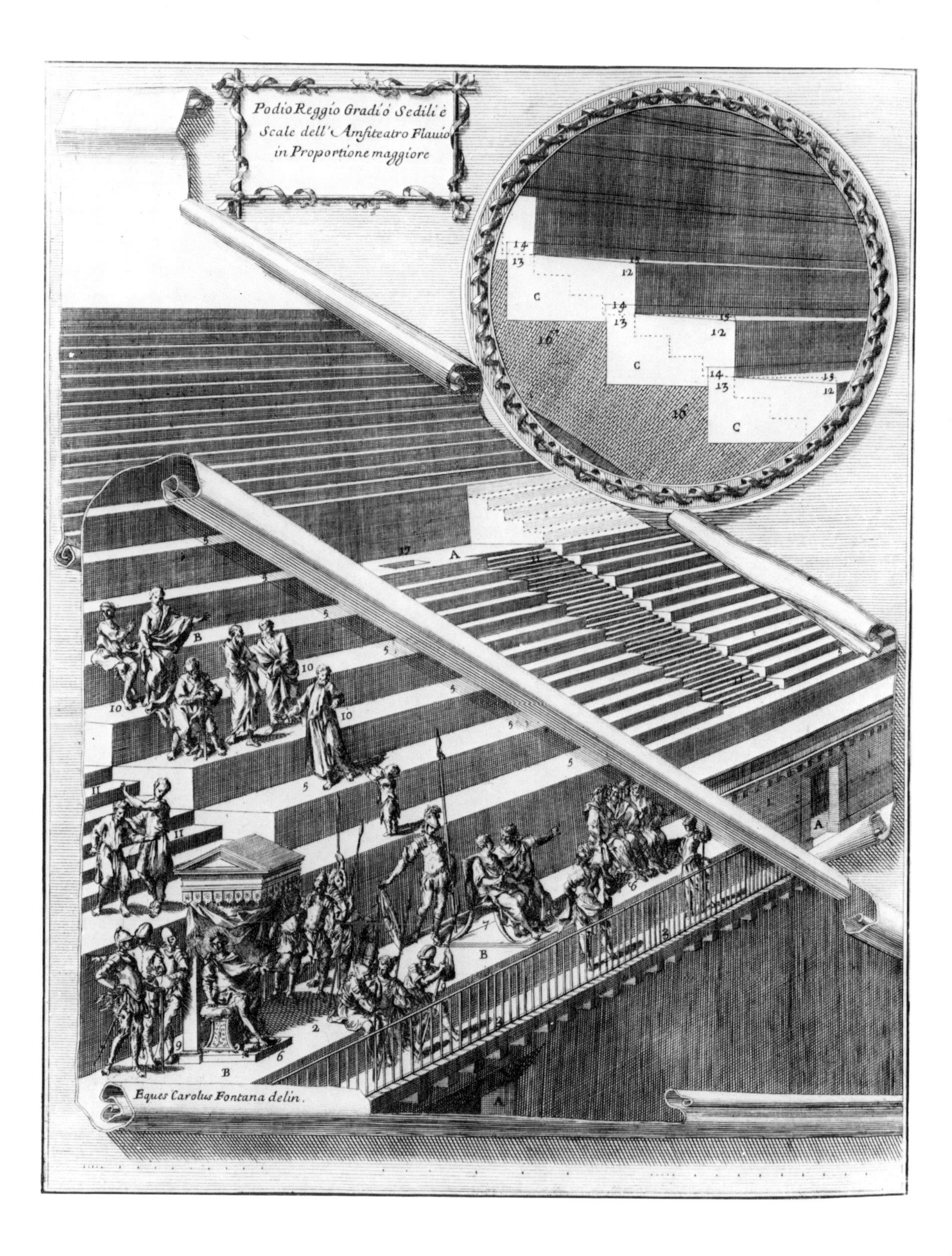
Podio Reggio Gradi ó Sedili é
Scale dell' Amfiteatro Flauio
in Proportione maggiore
Eques Carolus Fontana delin.

# V Construction

Sestertius of Titus, one of the very few Roman coins actually depicting the Colosseum.

Who designed the Colosseum? Until quite recently there was an old guide there who used to assure the tourists that the architect was a great Roman called Gaudentius who became a Christian and achieved martyrdom here in his own arena. This romantic theory was originally put forward by an eighteenth-century historian, Giovanni Marangoni, on the basis of a dubious interpretation of an equally dubious inscription in the crypt of the ancient Roman church of Santa Martina.

But the legend persisted long after Marangoni's scholarship was disproved. The Colosseum, more than most buildings, constantly raises this question of its authorship. As the romantic Signor Clementi put it in his book, *l'Anfiteatro Flavio*, published in 1912: 'When one marvels at this gigantic ruin, one's thoughts stray to the great architect who, through the force of his genius, conceived this titanic design and launched a challenge to the skies.'

On a more prosaic level too, the question of the architect's identity remains. The Colosseum is such a complex building that it is hard to study it without becoming conscious of the extreme intelligence and the originality behind it. This is a sophisticated masterpiece bearing the imprint of an extraordinary mind. Its architect is one of the lost geniuses of antiquity.

Why he is lost is something of a puzzle, although it is probably not necessary to descend to Marangoni's theory for an answer. As Mortimer Wheeler points out in his book on Roman architecture, 'creative Roman art and architecture, with vague and trivial exceptions, are anonymous'; the Roman patron had become the man who counted. Against the 'supreme personality-cult of the Emperor' the architect scarcely mattered. The

Fontana's impression of the imperial podium in the Colosseum, complete with the railing protecting it from the arena.

Romans are the faceless men of architecture, and the Colosseum represents the supreme example of the assertion of wealth and power over genius. One can almost see bull-necked old Vespasian, having won the mastery of the Roman world and paid for this great monument, treating the architect as one more imperial employee. The thought that he might share credit for his building with such a man almost certainly never entered his head.

And in a way, there is a rightness about this. The Colosseum is *his* building, tailor-made to serve *his* purpose. When it was built it was not beautiful as a self-sufficient work of art. It was a machine to help him rule, and much of its uniqueness came from qualities inherent in his empire – its scale, its purpose and the concentration of resources that it represented. This is state architecture with a vengeance, and it stands as an extraordinary portrait of the age it served.

Contemporary wall-painting of the amphitheatre at Pompeii, the oldest such structure still standing (see page 101).

The amphitheatre – the word was manufactured from two Greek words meaning 'theatre in the round' – was a machine that Rome invented for its own specific purposes. Previously the Roman showplaces were adapted from the Greek – the horseshoe-shaped theatre with the stage at one end, and the long thin stadium which was ideal for chariot-racing just as it had been for athletics. When Pompey built his great theatre in the first century BC it was still modelled on the Greek ideal. So was the stadium Vespasian's son, Domitian, laid out on what is now the site of the Piazza Navona in the Campus Martius. But the growing popularity of gladiators called for something different. During the late Republic the combats were held both in theatres and in the stadium of the Circus Maximus. Neither was ideal. In the theatre the view must have been restricted and the audience could not have felt genuine involvement with the fighting; while in the circus only Caesar's set-piece battle-scenes can have been effective. The niceties of individual combat would have been lost in so much space.

From the accounts of early combats it is clear that the Romans were trying to devise a way of showing them to best advantage. The place most frequently employed was the open space of the Forum, and there are descriptions of temporary stands erected, and wooden barriers built to keep spectators back. The effect must have been much like the main piazza of Siena today when it is crammed with people watching the horses race for the Palio. This would have been adequate for the occasional small show, although even then there were complaints from the people that the rich stands blocked their view. It must have been hazardous to stage fights against wild beasts in such conditions, and once gladiatorial combat started to become a full-blown ritual of the state, such *ad hoc* staging was inadequate.

The origins of the amphitheatre are distinctly vague. The oldest remaining one at Pompeii dates from the first century BC. Since Pompeii was originally much influenced by the Etruscans – who helped to make it an important gladiatorial centre of the South – it has been argued that this amphitheatre too must have derived from ancient Etruscan sources. On the other hand there is no evidence of anything resembling an amphitheatre on an Etruscan site – nor for that matter anywhere else in antiquity from this period – so that most archaeologists are content to describe it as an entirely Roman invention.

We have to rely on written sources for the earliest evidence of amphitheatres in Rome, and there is no way of checking or amplifying the brief details that survive. According to the Elder Pliny, Gaius Curio, a rich friend of Julius Caesar, built the first amphitheatre when giving sumptuous games in memory of his father. Hoping to impress his fellow-citizens he had an elaborate structure built of wood in the form of two semi-circular theatres, back to back. Together they held forty thousand people, and in the morning Curio gave two separate theatrical performances simultaneously for his guests. Then in the afternoon the two halves of the theatre were swung round on their axis. No one, Pliny insists, left his place while this went on, and when the halves had come together, forming a circle, Curio presented gladiatorial shows in the central arena.

This account of Pliny's has been disputed, mainly on grounds of sheer improbability. It would be hard enough with present-day technology and materials to operate this sort of conjuring-trick.

For the Romans, it is argued, such an achievement would have been impossible. However, Cicero provides confirmation of the story and, given what is known of the achievements of Rome's theatrical engineers, such an arrangement may quite well have worked. According to Pliny, this extraordinary machine actually functioned for two days. On the third, for some reason, no one dared risk turning it again – perhaps the weight of all those people had begun to tell – and the two halves were left joined as a permanent amphitheatre.

A near-contemporary of Curio, the even richer Marcus Scaurus, tried to outdo him on the sort of scale that Rome expected from its plutocrats. According to contemporary accounts, his amphitheatre was more permanent than Curio's. Constructed of marble, glass and gilded wood, it lacked its rival's somewhat alarming power to turn itself inside out, but it made up for this by holding, according to one estimate, eighty thousand people at a time. Its exterior dazzled the Romans with its bronze statues and 'artistic furnishings'. Like so much Roman public building, it was intended to impress. When it was finished, Scaurus is reported satisfied that he had outdone Curio and that no one would ever equal the size and splendour of his achievement.

He was underrating his successors and putting too great faith in glass and gilded wood. His showplace cannot have lasted long, but he and Curio had started a fashion and given the Roman amphitheatre a tradition of size and splendour that it never lost. From the beginning, it was a place of wonder, like some nineteenth-century fairground building on the grandest scale, suitably garish to attract the multitude and a fit setting for the Roman engineer's mechanical ingenuity.

There were to be at least four more attempts at building amphitheatres in Rome before the Colosseum. Caesar's was built quite simply of wood, and was put up in the Campus Martius for the special games he held at the dedication of his

Forum and the Temple of Venus. Unlike Scaurus' arena, it was not built to last; but the next one was. This was the stone amphitheatre built by Augustus' rich friend, Statilius Taurus; it was destroyed in Nero's fire. Piranesi claimed to have seen remains of it during the construction of the foundations of the Curia Innocenziana, but, like so many of the lost buildings of Augustan Rome, its true dimensions are a mystery. Augustus' reputed wish to build an amphitheatre of his own suggests that it was not adequate for the massive numbers of the full state games, and, although Caligula gave spectacles there, Dio Cassius reports that he too found it far too small. It must have been at this point that Caligula started the stone amphitheatre Suetonius describes, but which was never finished. Nero's wooden amphitheatre in the Campus Martius was an attempt to offer Rome a stop-gap for the full-scale amphitheatre that was needed.

Even the little that is known about these earliest amphitheatres serves to make clear the step Vespasian was taking with his plans for the Colosseum. These *ad hoc* buildings were being finally replaced by their permanent equivalents. Instead of wooden staging in the Campus Martius, the full power of architect and engineer was being used to turn the amphitheatre into a lasting setting for the full state ritual of Rome. Just as the emperors had already managed to transform gladiatorial combat into a state event, so they were now turning the amphitheatre into an institution to contain it. The skill of the architects was to produce a form which perfectly fulfilled the state's requirements, and which, in turn, provided the model for such buildings throughout the Empire.

The Colosseum is a good example of how effectively Rome's architects could work to serve Rome's emperors. They were not making splendid works of art; in terms of style their buildings usually appear derivative and are lumbering echoes of the ancient Greeks'. But they always showed an almost telepathic responsiveness to the desires of their rulers. At times it was as if the emperors spoke through them. Those endless public works – the Roman baths and aqueducts and market-places – with which the government bought popular support are witnesses to their architects' abilities. So are the temples, palaces, triumphal arches with which these rulers of the world proclaimed their splendour. To rule well was to build, and the great buildings of the city in their turn provide an extension of the imperial will – and nowhere more than the Colosseum.

Even the act of chosing such a site came as a gesture of Vespasian's power. Here in the fold between the Esquiline and

Roman builders at work. This detail of a relief now in the Lateran Museum shows builders employing a hoist of the type used to set up pillars in the Colosseum.

Caelian hills lay the waters of the deserted Stagna Nerone, that wonder of the Golden House, the lake which Nero had surrounded with his private vistas of dream villas, towns and landscaped countryside. Vespasian had already returned the land to the people and begun the destruction of the hated Golden House. Now he announced that he would build his amphitheatre for the Roman people here on the site of the lake itself. In one sweep he would obliterate a standing grievance against Nero, win popularity and gain for the Flavians the prestige of a prodigious feat.

The Colosseum started as a masterpiece of drainage. This was a skill the Romans had developed to an art, and the success of the Emperor's grandest gesture now depended on it. His architect's first problem was to free the site from water. He would have known by now of the existence of a firm underlying bed of gravel that would carry the foundations, and he constructed permanent stone sewers so successfully that they not only drained the lake into the Tiber, but guaranteed the dryness of the site in future. It was the sort of transformation scene that always appealed to the Romans, rather like the moment in a spectacle when the artificial lake was drained and gladiators continued fighting on the lake-bed. Overnight Nero's lake had disappeared. His follies were destroyed, and in their place Vespasian had his site where he could start to raise the massive walls of his great building.

In engineering there are clear affinities between the control of water and of human beings in the mass. In the preliminary designs for the Colosseum, similar foresight was applied to both. One reason why the building has stood for centuries can be attributed to the drainage system hidden beneath the main piers, a carefully constructed line of gullies leading the surplus water from the perimeter to the main sewer. In much the same way the architect devised a system to ensure that his vast amphitheatre would fill and empty perfectly with people. He did this by planning eighty so-called *vomitoria* – a word which graphically sums up the way the Colosseum spewed out its audience when the show was over – big numbered staircases leading the people to carefully segmented rows within the building. These staircases worked so efficiently that it has been calculated that a full audience could leave the building in three minutes flat.

During the actual show the problem was to keep everybody firmly in his place. The Roman crowd was not distinguished by its sense of order. Some sixty thousand of them were to be packed in tight and roused to near-hysteria by the sight of violence – this in the presence of the emperor, priests and upper classes. But their raw instincts had to be channelled so that the climax ended, not in destruction and riot, but in a sense of oneness with the emperor and the state. Again, this channelling was essentially an engineering problem, and everything depended on the form and the construction of the building.

This is where the real genius of the building lies. There is a splendid sureness in the way the architect banked mass on mass of human beings up from the arena to the high rim of the containing wall three hundred feet above the emperor's podium. Partly through density of numbers, partly through an extremely subtle disposition of the seating banks and the dividing walls, he could ensure that this would be a captive audience, kept in their places by the weight of people and the excitement that they generated.

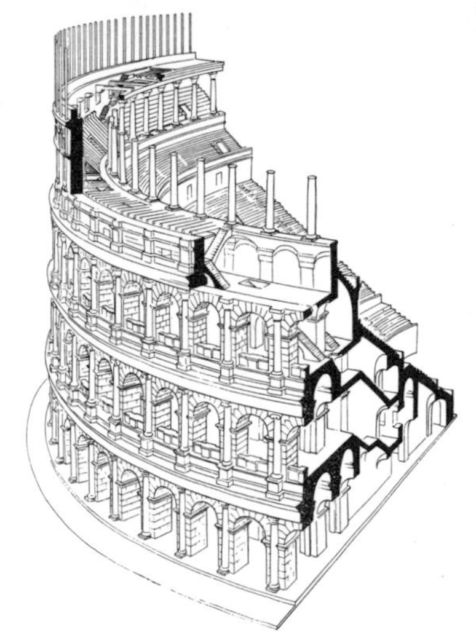

Segmented view of the construction of the Colosseum.

There was provision for additional control at vulnerable points. One such point was at the edge of the arena. Although the arena was some ten feet lower than floor level at the lowest seats, extra protection was provided by a surrounding wall just high enough to deflect a leaping animal but not to block the view from the seats behind. According to MacKendrick: 'Slots in the top of this wall are the postholes for a dismountable fence which supplied additional protection. Literary sources say it was of gilt metal surmounted by elephants' tusks. In front of the fence ran a cat-walk where archers were stationed to shoot beasts which got out of hand.' This absolutist building demonstrates the sort of social command the emperors exercised through their engineers.

Another point where there was provision for extra crowd control was above the podium. MacDonald has pointed out the special balconies from which the guard could fire upon rioters and protect the audience. Also, each stairway could be readily controlled by troops in case of riot; the greatest tribute to the architect's design lies in the complete absence of any record of the crowd getting out of hand during the whole history of the Colosseum.

In this it would be wrong to overlook the effect of the awe and splendour of the Colosseum itself. Unlike the previous Roman amphitheatres of wood, the actual building must have conveyed an unforgettable impression of solidity and power. The Empire was made manifest. The very building was a symbol of the emperor's strength. And at the same time it had been carefully arranged to provide the setting for an ordered image of the Roman state. Augustus had already shown how this was possible in his meticulous concern for dress, behaviour and strict placing by class and precedence in the theatre and the circus. This was to be exaggerated here. From the emperor on the podium to the humblest sailor from Trastevere working the billowing sunblind, the *velarium*, in the gods, everybody had his place. There were five separate seating areas. Each was kept quite distinct. However much Vespasian wanted to spoil his subjects, the elderly tax-farmer's son was not attempting to make this an egalitarian affair. The knights were seated in the front row by the arena. Senators were entitled to their place on the *pulvinar*, the raised balcony above. The emperor in majesty, surrounded by his favourites, the priests, the vestal virgins, occupied the imperial box. Behind him, class by class, the Roman people ascended the great curve of the *cavea*, each in the station to which it had pleased the ruler of the world to summon them.

Drawing by Fontana of the machinery designed to keep the Colosseum's immense sun-blind, the *velarium*, in place.

By the time work began on the Colosseum, Vespasian's building mania was already giving a face-lift to the city. He and his two sons were compulsive builders. Plutarch suggested that Domitian had 'a disease of building . . . and a desire, like Midas had, of turning everything to gold or stone'. Between them, these three Flavian emperors were responsible for over thirty major buildings in the city, including the great baths of Titus, Domitian's stadium and his enormous palace on the Palatine. It was an incredible burst of activity, evidence of the resources latent within the Roman Empire, and also of the importance that the emperors attached to these great public works.

Under Vespasian, Rome soon recovered the power and energy squandered by Nero. The ravages of Nero's fire were hurriedly restored, the Capitol rebuilt, and work was nearly finished on Vespasian's Temple of Peace and his new Forum.

Apart from prestige value for the dynasty, the Colosseum was a genuine attempt by Vespasian to give his subjects their share in the resurgent wealth of Rome. It was a way of offering a sort of luxury to the masses, as if the Golden House of Nero were being rebuilt for the Roman people. Vespasian had learned from Augustus the trick of strengthening his power through this sort of public gesture. And, unlike Augustus, Vespasian could really play the part of the bluff, middle-class old Roman inviting his fellow-citizens to share in the good things of Empire. Already he had opened his gardens on the Palatine to them, offered them the splendid libraries of his Forum, given the city its new temple and the restored Capitol. Now he was out to pamper them. When he opened up the Golden House it was not only the confiscated land that he was giving back to Rome. The Colosseum was to offer the people much the same images of fantasy and wealth that Nero had once created here for his own enjoyment – gilded corridors, elaborately painted ceilings, the whole interior gleaming with white marble. It was the earliest 'People's Palace' in the world. According to Calpurnius: 'The *zonae* [the walls dividing up the separate tiers] were studded with mosaics of precious stones; the awnings and the cushions were of silk, and fountains poured forth jets of perfumed water.'

The elaborate scenery and the arrangements for the changing stage sets which were to delight the crowd repeated the sort of visual fantasy that Nero loved. But behind all this illusion lay the iron sense of purpose of the Roman state. Not until modern times were rulers once more to command the sheer resources and the discipline that this one building represented.

Nobody knows exactly when work started. According to Burgess, it was immediately after Vespasian's return from the Jewish War in AD 75. Lipsius, arguing from the evidence of coins, thinks it was two years later. Either way, the sheer speed of building is phenomenal. For the Colosseum to have opened in the year AD 81, Vespasian's builders had between five and seven years to complete their work.

Admittedly, the Colosseum was by no means finished when Titus opened the inaugural games, although again there is uncertainty as to how far the work had reached. Middleton believed that up to Domitian's death the building stood no higher than the three orders of the arches of the façade, and that the amphitheatre was not complete until the third century AD, when the Emperor Septimius Severus restored widespread damage caused by fire and finished the fourth storey. On the other hand, brass coinage of Domitian, minted in AD 94, shows the Colosseum apparently complete with its fourth storey; at the inauguration the great bulk of the work must have been done.

It is hard to understand how much this meant in Roman terms. It has been worked out that it took 292,000 cartloads of travertine stone to build the external wall alone. It is also calculated that the building as a whole took over 750,000 tons of dressed stone, 8,000 tons of marble, 6,000 tons of concrete. Figures are hard to visualize and one gets a better picture of what all this involved when one realizes what has vanished. As it stands today, the Colosseum is what remains *after* the Romans had continually used it as a stone-quarry from the fall of the Empire until the Pope in 1597 officially banned the practice. By then it had generously provided stone for the rebuilding of St Peter's and several of the great Renaissance palaces.

In terms of bulk and sheer resources, the Colosseum is the approximate equivalent of three medieval cathedrals of the size of Salisbury. But the Flavian dynasty, unlike the Middle Ages, built in a hurry. Medieval man was happy building for the hereafter; Vespasian wanted his results at once. He intended to dedicate his amphitheatre before he died.

It is no coincidence that Vespasian was a painstakingly successful general. Much of the planning was conducted like the preparations for a full-scale military campaign. Here was the Roman military mind at work – methodical, remorseless and accustomed to getting things done on time and on the grandest scale. Vespasian set up a strong central authority to control his building programme, 'a ministry or office of works, presided over by a prefect', according to MacDonald. Without this, building on such a scale would have been impossible; the Colosseum was the product of that absolutist, centralized, military government Vespasian had inherited and made his own.

This shows continually in the organization behind the building and in the way the labour and resources were assembled at the site. Much of the success of the building was to depend on the sheer variety of raw materials employed. The architects could evidently draw on a sophisticated range of materials which they were to use with great precision – stone of varying weight and strength, brick, tile and concrete, quite apart from the accessories, such as marble, stucco, metal-work and wood, which were widely used in the finished building. To supply them on the necessary scale required a far-reaching organization. A special road was built to the quarries below Tivoli where the hard travertine stone was cut. The softer grey pepperino was quarried from below the Capitol, and the light volcanic rock seems to have been transported all the way from Praeneste. Marble from Luni and Carrara was shipped by sea along the coast and up the Tiber.

One fallacy about the Colosseum is that it was built by slaves. Possibly captives from the Jewish War were used as a labour force, digging foundations, levelling the site and working in the quarries. MacDonald estimates that up to two thousand captives of this sort could have been employed, but this is all.

Apart from all its sinister associations, the Colosseum is also a memorial to Roman craftsmanship. It was intelligence, not brutality, that raised it. The stone was cut and fitted by masons who knew their trade and took a pride in it. Much of the speed of construction was to depend on workmen who could take advantage of the developing technology of the Flavian builders. As with the materials involved, so with these workmen, one is impressed by their variety; more than a dozen workers' guilds are known to have been involved in the construction. These included *fabri*, construction workers, *fabri aerarii*, bronze-workers, *fabri ferrarii*, blacksmiths, *fabri lignarii*, carpenters, *figuli*, porters and brick-makers, *marmorarii*, marble-workers, *pavimentrarii*, pavement-layers, and *sectories serrarii*, masons.

The Emperor Septimius Severus (193–211), who in the third century rebuilt the Colosseum after the disastrous fire.

The immense building projects of the Empire seem to have relied upon a system under which labourers and craftsmen were organized in groups to which the individual worker bound himself. Traces of this system still persist in parts of Italy, where you can still find road-workers and porters organized as squads whose members bargain, work and are paid as a unit.

This system clearly suited an enormous project like the Colosseum. According to MacDonald, 'this shaping of manpower and knowledge into a system both orderly and flexible explains certain characteristics of the new architecture'. Certainly it explains how the Romans managed to organize a highly skilled, disciplined work force on the scale necessary to build the Colosseum.

It also to some extent refutes the idea that Rome's proletariat consisted of a parasitic mob of unemployed and unemployable living upon their wits and the imperial dole. On the contrary, Rome's artisans and craftsmen must have been more skilled and numerous than any in the ancient world, and, except for the long recession of Tiberius' reign, they must have found a regular source of employment from the emperor – and none better than from the Flavians. Like almost everything in Rome, the labour market depended on the emperor – and his continual building projects boosted the economy like any modern scheme of public works.

With the start of the work, one is again reminded of the Roman military mind at work. It was the military engineers who had first used standardization and prefabrication to achieve speed in their construction work. The Roman camp, the military town, had all been built according to a careful discipline and a strict geometric plan. So was the Colosseum. And as in all military architecture, this produced an instant sense of purpose. For all its bulk, the Colosseum might have been one of those indestructible forts or bridges thrown up by the Roman sappers under the noses of the enemy.

Throughout the period of building, the officials of Vespasian's Ministry of Works must have worked frantically to keep a steady flow of the required materials on time. Indeed, the whole rate of construction must have depended on the efficiency and toughness of these men. The Colosseum is the product of a skilled bureaucracy. There was no room or time for much of the normal building work to be done *in situ*. Instead whole operations – the cutting of pillars, finishing of capitals, dressing of stone – were performed elsewhere, so that the work on site could be immensely simplified, much of it confined to skilful assembly of materials at speed.

The effect of this can still be seen throughout the building. There was no time for inessentials, and it is clear that what mattered here was over-all effect, rather than time-consuming detail. Much of the surviving carving lacks finish and refinement – as one would expect from masons doing mass-production work under pressure. Middleton has pointed out the particularly coarse mouldings of the imposts of the inner square piers on the ground floor, and also the awkward way they had been cut. Similar examples abound, but at the same time the construction work rarely falters. In things that mattered nothing was left to chance.

For all his vigour and robustness Vespasian was aging. He was already in his sixties when the work began. If he were to achieve his ambition and dedicate his amphitheatre in the name of his dynasty before he died, there was no time to lose. The work pressed on. No building of this size, even in Rome, had grown at such a pace.

It was this need for speed that seems to have dictated its

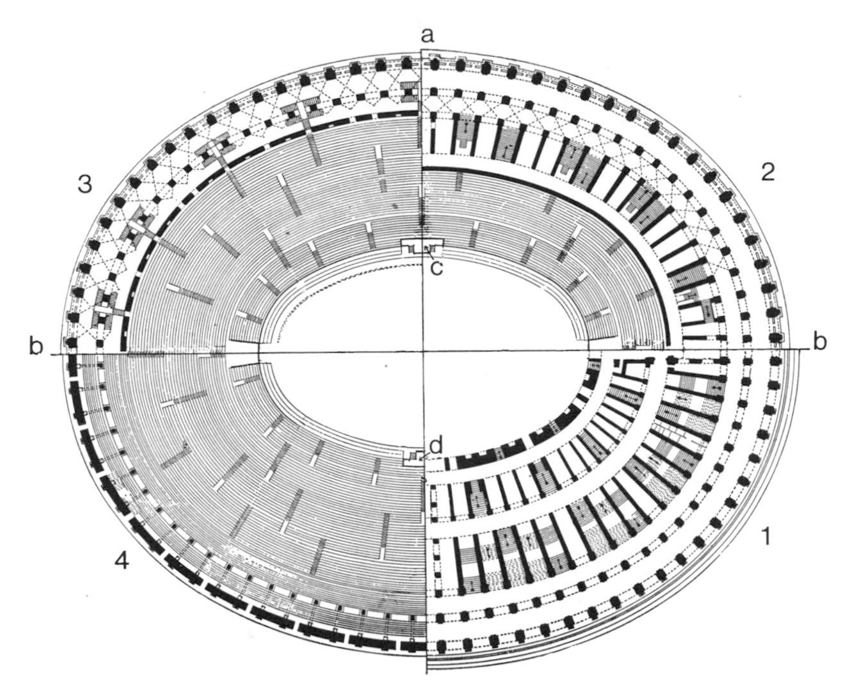


Composite plan of the four storeys (1 – 4) of the Colosseum showing the position of the emperor's entrances (a), gladiators' entrance (b), emperor's box (c) and consul's box (d).

design. The architect was ruled by the necessity of harnessing the full resources of his work force. The result was the nearest thing Rome ever got to the style and methods of large-scale twentieth-century building. In many ways the architect was fortunate. Despite the earlier attempts, an amphitheatre was a new form in Roman building, calling for new methods of construction. To build at all on such a scale as this, he had to innovate. He did so with great daring, taking advantage of his men and his materials and using them with the flexibility of an artist and the decisiveness of a general. The aim was to produce the ancient world's first instant large-scale building.

Every advantage was exploited. Even the lake-bed site proved useful. Once it was drained, the saucer-shaped depression saved shifting more than 200,000 cubic metres of top-soil for the foundations. These foundations were then sunk eighteen feet into the gravel. Once in place, the work could hurry on with the essential core of the building – the eighty radial walls converging from the perimeter on to the arena like the straight spokes of an enormous wheel. These walls were to support the rows of vaults, which bore the main *cavea* of the amphitheatre, with its sloping tiers of marble seats. It was a very modern concept, quite unlike the normal Roman practice of putting all the strength into the outer fabric of a building. This was a form of frame construction. Its elegant geometry could translate perfectly into the steel girdering of today. As it was, with these radial walls, the builders managed to achieve exactly the same adaptation of strength to weight that a skilled modern architect would calculate. They did this through a subtle variation in the materials employed. Near the arena, where the wall was lowest and had least to bear, it was constructed of soft concrete made of mixed rubble of brick and *tufa* limestone. Five yards back, as the wall rises and the weight it bears is heavier, the concrete changes and is made of the hard lava, *silex*, that was used on Roman roads. Then comes a pier of solid travertine stone built into the wall for extra strength, while near to the perimeter, where height and weight are greatest, the radial wall is built entirely of massive blocks of *tufa*, some of them up to six feet long.

These radial walls were really the key to the construction of the Colosseum. Not only did they bear the main weight of the *cavea*, but they also had to play an important part in the actual building work. Indeed, the use made of them is one of the ingenious features of the builders' plan. Once in place, the walls enabled extremely heavy blocks of stone to be hoisted and then set in place along the outer wall. More important, they were made to carry scaffolding (the sockets for which can be seen in places) on which an immense platform was constructed. Thanks to this, work could go forward on two levels – an effective doubling of activity on the site – and as the outer walls were finished, the pace was ruthlessly maintained, with workmen operating shifts to keep to the schedule of the Emperor's declining days.

Thanks to the building's perfect symmetry and the architect's standardization of components, the tempo actually increased at this stage. Stair-treads were standardized, for instance (throughout the whole building they are the same measurement). So were the marble seats for the spectators (on a set basis of twenty-three inches per individual). As a further means of simplifying all construction, measurements were made in fixed units of the so-called *modula*. The *modula* was five Roman feet – wherever possible, fractions were avoided. Also, towards the latter stage of the construction, the builders increasingly resorted to speedier methods. This was quite possible once the massive stone blocks of the outer walls had been fixed in position and the laborious work of locking them in place with iron cramps was finished. Concrete was used now on a scale unprecedented in any Roman building. For the vaults carrying the *cavea*, and for the vaulted roofs of all the corridors, it was run liquid over wooden centring. This was an innovation that produced lightness of construction and saved valuable time.

By the year AD 80 the bulk of the Colosseum was all but finished – so was Vespasian. It must have been a haunting moment when the old Emperor-God was carried in to dedicate the towering walls and barely finished archways of his great design. This building, more than all his other works combined, symbolized the great achievements of the dying Emperor – the sense of purpose he had restored to the imperial government, the order he had given to the Roman world, the massive power he had wielded. Few men have ever left the world on such a scale.

Yet at the same time the whole building served as a reminder of the price that Rome would pay for this: the exploitation of the lowest human instincts – cruelty, vulgarity, hysteria – and all to guarantee a show of popular support for the emperors' military dictatorship.

This is one reason why the Colosseum seems an ambiguous memorial, simultaneously recalling both the proudest and the most disgusting qualities of Rome. And similarly it is hard to give a final judgment on its merits as a building. The Colosseum was two separate things – the tasteless product of a tasteless age, and a great functional construction.

As has been pointed out before, the Colosseum is at its best seen as a ruin. When the four storeys of the smoothly stuccoed outer wall were finished, it must have looked top-heavy with the great mass of the unbroken rim looming oppressively above the squat pillars of the lower storey. Time and the stone thieves have improved things here; by demolishing so much of the outer wall, they have reduced the over-all proportions, and have brought a touch of picturesque irregularity to the whole building. More important, they have stripped it totally of its expensive trappings. It must have been a monstrous place, with all those acres of white marble, those niches filled with statuary, the fountains and the gilded ceilings – Hollywood historical in a Roman setting. The carving and the decoration that survive are not encouraging. Writing about the pillars and capitals of the outer wall, one recent historian has said; 'The Greek orders are simply *appliqués* on a Roman mass; the columns themselves have as much relation to the building as those which used to adorn the steel-framed hotels of the 1930s.'

Mumford is very scathing on the subject too, objecting in particular to the need the Romans felt to clothe the Colosseum in so much vulgar decoration. This is for him quite typical of the overblown hypocrisy of the early Empire – 'nakedness for the Roman was either an accompaniment to defecation or a prelude to lust'.

The Colosseum as the modern tourist sees it. He can appreciate the logic and stark splendour of the great building.

But as it stands today, the vast interior of the Colosseum could hardly be more naked, and one sees what no Roman crowd saw – the bare geometry of the construction. One can appreciate the daring and the scale of the endeavour. Here in its ruined state it is as if the building had been sectionalized to

demonstrate the sweep of the enormous radial walls, the height of the outer rim, the logic of the corridors and the connecting arches. As well as the sadism and the hypocrisy of Rome, logic and daring and a sense of purpose also had their place in that extraordinary civilization.

Roman lamp depicting a gladiator's equipment – greaves, shield, knives and dagger.

# VI Gladiators

As the games grew into purposive state rituals under the early Empire, the whole institution of Rome's gladiators had to keep pace with them. The gladiators' status rose – so did their numbers. The organization that supplied and trained them rapidly became more complex and efficient. The cult of gladiators spread through the Roman world until, as Friedländer wrote, whenever Romans of any class drew breath, 'they breathed in the passion for the circus and the arena'.

Even emperors like Caligula and Hadrian tried their luck as combatants, and Commodus, whose proudest boast was his skill as a gladiator, was widely rumoured to have been fathered by a Roman *hoplomache*. (Commodus, incidentally, claimed over a thousand victories in the arena; only death stopped him carrying out his plan of being sworn in for his final term as consul in a gladiator's uniform.)

Commodus was clearly an extreme case, but the steady social rise of gladiators under the Empire was remarkable; it helped to make them baffling figures even to the Romans, who never quite made up their minds about them. One finds them in one breath treating gladiators as *dishonestae personae*, the lowest of the low, and classing them along with whores and Christians as not even worthy of a decent burial. Then the next moment they are imperial favourites, darlings of the crowd, fêted in public, and in private treated like the famous gladiator from Pompeii who was *sospirium puellarum*, 'the dream of all the girls'.

The gladiator became an expression of the splendour and tradition of the Empire. Helmet from Naples embossed with allegorical figures representing Rome and its submissive provinces.

The basis of the gladiatorial cult lay primarily in slavery – in the ancient right of the slave-owner to dispose of his human chattels as he wished. The gladiator-bands that caused such havoc in the city during the late Republic were directly owned by their rich Roman masters. J.P.V.D. Balsdon has written that

Gladiatorial games being popular, vote-winning events, candidates for office acquired bands of gladiators (borrowing money heavily for the purpose if they could not afford the expense) in order to give games. . . . The games over, the survivors were sold to another politician who had similar ambitions, or they might be employed as a formidable bodyguard for their employer as he moved about the streets.

Such gladiator-slaves had essentially the same relationship to their master as the more conventional household slaves. This was so even with the armies of gladiators built up by Pompey and Caesar; Antony's gladiators, destined originally for the arena at Alexandria, proved so loyal to him that they were the last of all his men to stand by him after defeat at Actium.

On a more mundane level, gladiator-slaves were also regarded as a sage investment. Cicero wrote to the wealthy Atticus: 'I hear that your gladiators are wonderful fighters. If you had wanted to hire them out you would have recovered your expenses in a couple of games.'

Good fighting gladiators were in permanent demand. They could be bought and sold like ordinary slaves, and ownership implied the unquestioned right to compel them to enter the arena. Not until the more humane climate of the Emperor Hadrian's reign in the second century AD was a law passed forbidding a slave from being sold to the arena without just cause – in the same breath the Emperor banned female slaves from being sold to brothels. Before this, even emperors had been known to dispose of unwanted male slaves as gladiators. Vitellius made Asiaticus, a former slave, his catamite and favourite. Suetonius reports that: 'However, Asiaticus behaved so insolently, and so thievishly as well, that Vitellius sold him to an itinerant trainer of gladiators; but impulsively bought him back when he was just about to take part in the final match of a gladiatorial contest.' Shortly after, Asiaticus was presented by the Emperor with the gold ring of knighthood.

Even under the later Empire, consignment to the arena remained a real threat for a household slave. The Emperor Macrinus was described sending his runaway slaves to the arena on recapture, and in the *Satyricon*, Petronius tells a cruel anecdote about a Roman matron. When one of her male slaves refused to sleep with her, she told her husband that he had tried to rape her and had him instantly condemned to the arena where he died.

Slavery also helped produce the necessary callousness and blanket inhumanity which allowed the Roman world to stomach the arena. Only a society conditioned to see slaves as inferior beings could have accepted the death of countless gladiators quite so complacently. Seneca was virtually alone when he complained in the middle of the first century AD of the inhumanity of the butchery in the arena. Otherwise, the shows seem to have caused no affront to Roman consciences.

The conventional wisdom of this slave-owning world could not admit a universal right of life; rights, like everything in Rome, were graded by rank and status. The unquestioned inferiority of slaves was one of the foundations of the Roman world. As Seneca explained, the owner had a perfect right to starve his slave, to beat him, depilate him, force him to satisfy his unnatural lusts. If a slave murdered his master, the law prescribed the automatic execution of all the other slaves in the household as an example and deterrent. With this background of disposable human life there was no reason for the arena to arouse disquiet.

While the gladiators must be seen as members of a slave society, they were outside the day-to-day master and slave relationships of the time. From the start, their role as licensed killers gave them their own uneasy status – they had to swear a special oath, they wore their distinctive uniforms and were regarded as a potential source of danger to society. As their importance and their numbers grew under the Empire, so they soon formed a virtual caste, with their own laws, their own cult and distinct organizations marking them off quite clearly from all other groups and classes in the state.

This process was remarkable, and happened in response to a continuing demand for well-trained gladiators both from the government and from society at large. Quite how this happened is less clear. Somehow the Roman world evolved a system that produced a steady stream of trained men in their prime, prepared to fight and kill each other as part of the Empire's favourite spectator sport. This system stands as terrifying proof of the efficiency of Rome.

Even in the late Republic ordinary slaves could never have supplied sufficient men for the arena, and the majority came from the human surplus of the time. They were already marked out for disposal by the time they reached the arena.

The most common source of all was the hordes of prisoners captured by Rome's triumphant armies. As Friedländer writes: 'As the Empire expanded, the natives of the confines were dragged into the Roman arena. During the Republic, Gauls, Thracians, Samnites were seen fighting; under the Empire, the

Gladiators as decoration. A *secutor* and a Negro *retiarius* carved in ivory on the handle of a second-century knife.

tattooed savages of Britain, the fair Germans of the Rhine and Danube, the dusky Moors from the Atlas, African Negroes and Sarmatian Arabs.'

There was no obligation on a victorious general to treat vanquished enemies with mercy. According to whim and circumstance, a defeated army could be pardoned, slaughtered or sold off as booty. During his Gallic Wars, Caesar normally found it expedient to pardon prisoners on condition that they laid down their arms and swore an oath of fealty to Rome. This did not stop him bringing numbers of prisoners to Rome – his Gallic swordsmen and British charioteers. After the fierce fighting of the Jewish War, Vespasian could not risk further trouble from the remnants of the defeated Jewish army. Prisoners were a problem which he solved by consigning half of them to the living death of the Egyptian mines, and the others to the arenas of Asia Minor. In Aurelian's triumph there marched captured Goths, Alani, Roxolani, Sarmatians, Franks, Suevi, Vandals, Germans, Palmyrenes and Egyptian rebels, followed by ten Gothic amazons – most of them destined for the arena.

As well as being a convenient way of disposing of unwanted prisoners-of-war, the arena was also made the official place of execution for Rome's basest criminals – men whose crimes were held to have deprived them of all human rights and who were guilty of murder, robbery, sacrilege, mutiny or arson. The arena was theoretically a deterrent – rather like Tyburn – and in executing these criminals Roman ingenuity was free to devise new forms of cruelty. Antiquity was never squeamish over the punishment of criminals. In Rome, arson had previously been punished by burning or suffocation, parricide by public disembowelment; spies were blinded. Now the need to give the audience an unforgettable example led to some hideous refinements.

The normal practice was to have criminals executed by fully armed gladiators – *damnati ad gladium* (this would take place before the full-scale combats of the day) – or else to throw them straight to the wild beasts – *damnati ad bestias*. Despite the fate of Androclus, who survived because a lion recognized him as the man who previously removed a thorn from his paw, the chances of the criminal surviving were remote.

Towards the end of the Republic, this began to change as the arena started to need all the criminals it could get. One tendency was for condemned men to be used in the arena purely for the sadistic titillation of the audience. Under Caligula and Commodus such men were forced to play as actor-victims in grotesque re-enactments of episodes in Roman history. These were extremely popular. One criminal, cast as Mucius Scaevola, had to hold his hand in a brazier of live coals in imitation of the ancient hero. Another, cast as Hercules, ended his performance writhing in genuine agony upon a pyre.

As the demand for shows increased, so criminals also became an important source of actual gladiators. Originally it had been a normal practice to sell condemned men to the holders of games on condition that they were killed within a certain period – usually three months. Gradually it became more usual to consign such men to the gladiator schools for training – *damnati in ludum*. The motive for this important change seems to have lain purely in the interests of the games. It would be wishful thinking to detect in it a softening of heart towards the victims.

This bronze statuette of a gladiator was probably used as a candle-holder.

The rate at which men found themselves condemned to the gladiator schools seems to have varied with the demand for manpower and the imperial whim. In the provinces, even in the days of the Republic, it was a fairly common grievance to hear of men unjustly punished in this way. Cicero blamed Caesoninus, proconsul in Macedonia, for dispatching numbers of innocent men to fight wild beasts. In Spain, Lucius Balbus the Younger tried as quaestor to force a Roman citizen called Fadius to fight as a gladiator. When Fadius refused, he was burned alive in the local gladiator school.

The actual training that the criminal received once he had been *damnatus in ludum* seems to have varied too – again a great deal must have depended on the current demand from the shows. According to Suetonius' account of Claudius' sea-fight on Lake Fucine, the several thousand 'gladiators' involved were criminals armed and dressed for the part and obviously expecting pardon as the reward for a good day's fighting. Tacitus states that there were nineteen thousand men on each side. Even if this is a considerable over-estimate, it is hard to credit that there were so many men in Rome all simultaneously guilty of some serious crime. What is more likely is that every available criminal capable of wielding a sword was brought in. Minor offenders must have found themselves conscripted for the Emperor's festival. Certainly the men's behaviour on that day – their blank refusal to start fighting after the sarcastic comment of the Emperor's – hardly suggests the mien of well-trained gladiators.

A happening like this was obviously exceptional, but the fact is that, from the late Republic onwards, an increasing number of criminals were compelled to fight as gladiators and trained for the part. The gladiator's world was tailor-made for them; a murderer became a hero in the arena, and many criminals found success there, often achieving fame and even freedom through the sword. Against considerable odds, major criminals were known to survive to earn the *rudius*, the wooden sword of honourable discharge, after three years. Others are found who stayed on voluntarily, finding the life agreeable.

The Roman state produced the manpower and sanctioned its use in the arena, but the key to the developed system of Rome's gladiators lay in the elaborate arrangements made for training and distributing them. This system grew until it formed a network covering the Empire. As it gradually developed it was to provide a unique example of the effective interplay of private initiative, state enterprise and large-scale Roman capitalism.

Although gladiators continued to be owned by wealthy individuals like Atticus, there were not sufficient men like him to provide the supply of trained gladiators needed by the arenas. As early as the beginning of the first century BC this was already being taken over by the businessmen. Rome was the temple of the profit motive. Scarcely had gladiators started to fight at funerals than there were men around them eager to make a fortune from their blood. These enterprising men were known as *lanistae*. The word is thought to have derived from the Etruscan word for 'butcher'. According to Carcopino: 'These contractors, whose trade shares in Roman law and literature the same infamy that attaches to that of the pander or procurer, were in sober fact Death's middlemen.'

Despite the odium attached to their trade – the poet Martial coupled their role with that of libellous informers and liars – they offered the Roman public an invaluable service. They were a cross between a modern theatrical agent and a travelling showman, touring the Roman world with their troupes of gladiators and ready to mount a show for anybody who could pay. Some became wealthy and could guarantee top-rate performers; one *lanista* grandly described himself as 'business manager of a gladiatorial troupe' – *negotiator familiae gladiatoriae*. This would have been the sort of man to whom Vitellius sold Asiaticus. Other *lanistae* had to struggle for a living with a collection of fifth-rate gladiators, touring the provinces rather like the owner of a fairground boxing-booth. Petronius describes just such a troupe of gladiators – 'a wretched, weedy, two-penny-halfpenny lot, who would drop down as soon as look at them'.

Managing gladiators of this sort was a chancy business.

Wastage rates were high. There is an account of one *lanista* offering nineteen gladiators, only one of whom was actually his own – the remainder had all been lent to him by other owners.

Under the Empire men of this sort were quite incapable of providing gladiators in sufficient quantity and quality to satisfy the requirements of state and of sophisticated audiences. Something more organized was needed.

Some of the Roman gladiator schools were of considerable antiquity. They first appeared in Campania, that land to the south of Rome which had once been an Etruscan colony and was the traditional home of gladiators. It was at Capua in Campania in 73 BC that Spartacus, a Thracian slave, organized a break-out from a gladiator school where he was captive and with seventy comrades started his slave rebellion in the South. This was the one occasion when gladiators rebelled against their lot and caused society serious trouble. For a while they defended the lower slopes of Vesuvius. They were joined by countless disaffected slaves. When they defeated one army sent to capture them they forced their would-be captors to fight as gladiators to amuse them. When they were finally put down by Crassus and ten Roman Legions, every captured rebel was crucified along the road from Capua to Rome.

The Spartacus revolt must have increased the fear in which society held these warlike outcasts in its midst. It must also have made the régime in these gladiator schools, against which Spartacus rebelled, still harsher. There was strict security over gladiators' weapons, which by law had to be locked in the armoury when not in use. Some gladiator schools seem to have been more like penal settlements than training centres. In Pompeii, the most gruesome sight remains the punishment building attached to the town's gladiator school. When it was excavated, six shackled skeletons were found in the cells.

But it is interesting that, despite the enormous damage Spartacus and his gladiators inflicted on central Italy, there was no question afterwards of closing the gladiator schools. However dangerous they might be, the Romans knew they were essential if gladiatorial games were to continue. They were also highly profitable and, already, important Romans were investing in them.

Bronze statuette of a dwarf dressed as a gladiator in the stocks. Gladiators also appealed to the Roman taste for the grotesque.

Sarcophagus depicting two gladiators challenging each other. Their seconds stand beside them, holding spare weapons.

(*Below*) the gladiator barracks at Pompeii and (*right*) the amphitheatre at Pompeii as it is today. Vesuvius looms in the background.

In his novel *The Gladiators*, Arthur Koestler gives a convincing picture of a typical owner of such a school, a wealthy *nouveau-riche* called Lentulus, a politically influential Roman who comes from Rome to Capua to set up his training school.

His business connections spread, net-like, all over Italy and the provinces; his agents buy the human material at the Deli slave-market and sell it, transformed into model gladiators, to Spain, Sicily and the Asiatic courts after one year's thorough training.

The schools not only trained gladiators – they also tended to by-pass the *lanistae* by hiring out gladiators directly to important patrons. This seems to have been done on a clear sale-or-return basis, the school's owner receiving a capital sum for any of his men killed. Those who survived had to be sent back promptly to the school, along with an agreed fee for their services. Throughout the first century BC such schools did well and steadily increased in number. For, despite the disorders of the time, business activity was flourishing throughout the Roman world; as banking centre of the world, Rome was full of men with capital to invest. With their high profits and expanding markets, the gladiator training schools inevitably attracted them. Thus they became one area in which three crucial elements of Roman life could fruitfully combine – its slavery, its ebullient capitalism and its unrivalled powers of organizing human beings.

The size and continuity of these training schools helps to explain the role they played in Roman life. Some were enormous – they had to be to supply men on the scale the Empire needed.

Floor mosaic showing the various types of gladiator fighting in the arena.

The school which Caesar owned at Capua possessed armour for five thousand fighters, yet on top of this he tried to set up further schools, including one at Rome. The training school excavated at Pompeii – a modest one by the standards of the time – includes an impressive barracks block, a training square, a sanatorium and the prison where the skeletons were found. Each school was also the centre of a thriving industry – tailors and cobblers and armourers, as well as masseurs and medical men. Galen, the most celebrated anatomist of antiquity, started his medical career as doctor to a school in Asia Minor. (His work gave him a unique field of study in the treatment of wounds and the dissection of corpses.) These gladiator-doctors also paid great attention to the men's diet, attempting to produce hardness of muscle and the greatest staying-power.

But the real work of the schools centred round the day-to-day routine which was to turn this human raw material into trained gladiators. The beginners started like recruits in the army. Armed with a wooden sword (*lusoria arma*), they all went through a general course of combat, learning the standard thrusts and parries against wooden figures. This part of the instruction was conducted by retired gladiators, and during this period the recruit was carefully watched. Whichever style of gladiator he became depended on the aptitude he showed. After the intial stage, the gladiator was trained exclusively by type. Each style of fighting had its special trainers – *doctor myrmillonum*, *doctor Thraecum* and so on. At least sixteen different types of gladiator have been distinguished, but they fell broadly

A Thracian gladiator holding his distinctive round shield and scythe-like dagger.

into five categories – the *eques*, mounted fighters; *essedarii*, charioteers; the *Galli*, *myrmillones*, *hoplomachi*, *Samnites* and *secutores*, all of them heavily armed fighters; the *Thraeces*, lightly armed men, and the *retiarii*, with their nets and tridents.

During this second stage of training the novices would fight each other with their wooden swords; then, at a crucial point, would come the moment when they fought *decretoria arma*, with real swords. At the big schools the gladiators would be divided into two main classes, the old hands, the *veterani* who had experienced the arena, and the *tirones*, who had still to fight their first duel in earnest.

Despite the capital investment they represented, gladiators were treated rough. The staple diet of the training school was beans and barley; discipline was harsh, punishment severe. Sleeping-cells at Pompeii were barely twelve feet square. On top of this there was the risk of serious injury during training and the perpetual shadow of ultimate death in the arena. And yet the gladiators seem to have accepted this régime.

True, penalties for desertion were severe, and the security arrangements in the schools were taken seriously – particularly after the Spartacus revolt. For some while new schools were set up away from towns or on small islands. But by the beginning of the Empire one gets the feeling that these gladiator factories were no longer regarded as quite the social threat that they had been. By the end of the first century AD there were four of them in Rome, yet the nearest thing to a mutiny that happened there was when fifty freshly captured Saxon prisoners strangled each other in the night rather than face each other in the arena. These were untrained men. With the real gladiators there is no evidence that they were treated as a source of danger or disorder under the Empire. No one attempted to revive those bad old habits of using them as private armies or bodyguards to lead a *coup d'état*. There was only one real repetition of those depressing days under the late Republic when gladiators earned a bad name by the havoc that they caused on the streets of Rome. This was when the Emperor Nero led them in person on his nocturnal roistering, beating up honest citizens and robbing their houses.

This lapse must be attributed to Nero's sense of fun rather than to the wildness of the gladiators. Apart from this, their conduct was exemplary. Until the final banning of their combats by the Emperor Constantine in the fourth century, the Empire's gladiators did their duty and behaved like conscientious members of society.

This was the achievement of the schools, and an incredible achievement it was. Rome is remembered for its laws, its roads, its universal government. It should also be remembered for its continuing success at turning the unwanted manpower of the Empire into this docile army of dedicated gladiators. The schools did this through a precise awareness of the psychology of the performer and the fighting man. The conditioning was subtle, ruthless and complete. In its essentials it appears extremely modern.

From the beginning, the prime aim of the schools was to instil into a new recruit the sense of belonging to an élite marked out by toughness from an effete society. The gladiators had their own god, Mars, and there was a carefully fostered *esprit de corps* throughout the school. The oath sworn on admission – to submit to being scourged with rods, burned with fire and killed with steel – must have given an impressive sense of joining an esoteric brotherhood. (There are strong overtones here of the admission ceremonies to the widespread mystery religions of the time.) And the recruit was also welcomed to the burial societies which the gladiators were encouraged to form among themselves. Professor Grant has written: 'Gladiators were formed into an elaborate hierarchy, rising at the top of each branch to the rank of *primus palus* or first-class fighter. Each school and every branch of the profession within the school had its first, second, third and fourth grades and these were accommodated in separate halls.'

The early months of training in the schools show constant similarities with present-day army basic training. There was the same regard for fitness, graduated hardship and for using drill to turn the individual into a purposeful automaton. The Younger Pliny was highly critical of one training school he visited where only one recruit in ten could face a sword thrust to the eyes without blinking. During this stage of training, the veteran instructors played a key role as models for the uninitiated. Within the closed society of the schools, these powerful survivors must have enjoyed considerable prestige. These were the men who knew it all – the tricks, the stories, the traditions. From these old hands the novice would have picked up something of the lore and legends of the gladiators – stories of men like the great Musclosus, known as Hercules, and Spiculus, who fought his way to become Nero's favourite and ended up with villas and slaves and gladiators of his own. These legends were shot through with hope – it is with hope that men sustain themselves – and every gladiator must have

A bare-headed *retiarius*.

Gladiator carrying the big oblong shield of a *hoplomachus*.

known of the time the Emperor Domitian stopped the fight between two gladiators, declaring that each had fought so well that each should have the palm of victory and the wooden sword of honour.

The veteran gladiators who told such stories had come through safely. As instructors they were encouraging their pupils to share their prowess. Think of a recruit's reaction. For the trainee gladiator the only hope of victory and survival lay in the absolute perfection of his skill. This perfection had to become a total way of life. In comparison with this, the demands made upon a modern athlete by his trainer seem almost self-indulgent.

The routine within the schools was carefully arranged to lead the trainee naturally towards his first encounter in the arena – again that Roman thoroughness. Each stage of training had its goal – the first time the recruit was permitted to fight in combat with the wooden sword after the weeks of practice, the day when he was chosen for the honour of becoming a *Samnite* or a *hoplomachus* or a *retiarius*, the moment when he fought his trial duel with a naked sword.

The training schools had their own practice arenas – that of the excavated Ludus Maximus in Rome is nearly half the size of the arena in the Colosseum and had seats for visitors. Gladiators were watched, applauded, studied during training. Real devotees of the games attended their trial combats rather as racing men today spot form at yearling trials.

And so the day the gladiator entered the arena for the first time for public combat came as the culmination of the whole year's work. Here was no cowed wretch thrust trembling to his doom. He had been thoroughly conditioned for this moment. His trainer's words would be in his ears, and the great audience waiting for him. After the rough life of the training school, he was now superbly clad. The night before, in contrast with the usual diet of the barracks, he had been feasted like the Emperor himself. All eyes were on him. This was his chance to prove himself and put his hard-won skill to the test. He was engaging in the most exciting game of all and gambling his life against his opponent's. For this brief moment this rejected man could feel himself part of the splendour of the Empire, and it is hard to think of any thrill to equal that of victory – the sheer relief, the mass applause, the palm presented by the Emperor. One can understand why champion gladiators frequently refused the *rudius*. Seneca heard a gladiator actually complaining of the dearth of shows during Tiberius' reign:

'Soon all my youth will be gone and I will have lost my chance of fame for ever.'

The gladiator schools were gradually changing the whole character of the shows, shifting the emphasis from those early spectacles of execution and ritual sacrifice towards a modern-style mass sport. This was a complex evolution, and by its very nature it could never be complete. There would always be a basis of compulsion and a strong punitive element towards the contestants in the arena. There would be times too when the arena became the scene for indiscriminate and mindless slaughter. But at the same time, the influence of the schools was all towards making the shows exciting popular events with much the same appeal as a contemporary prizefight or soccer international. The games were being turned into a game.

The first way this came about was through the development of style and skill in fighting. The mere presence of those veteran instructors in the gladiator schools guaranteed an element of gamesmanship even within the bloodiest encounter. These veterans taught by rule. They established an accepted expertise among the gladiators. This in its turn was picked up and appreciated by the audiences. Even by Caesar's day it was sufficiently established for him to have been able to send his gladiators for their training to private masters-of-arms in Rome. Under the Empire, as Friedländer wrote, 'children played at gladiators, as they do now in Andalusia at bull and matador. Adolescence was passionately addicted to the gladiators, who were a staple stop-gap in the conversation, and proverbs sprang from the arena.'

Rules, lore and expertise – these are all vital elements in sport. But there were still two facts which seem to prevent us from regarding a gladiatorial combat as a game – death, and the unfree status of the contestants. It is significant that on both these scores the gladiator schools made efforts to disguise or blur the reality of what was happening. Careful conditioning in the gladiator schools helped to produce what still appears the strangest and most chilling feature of the gladiators – their cult of dying, the equivalent of the cool impersonal way a matador is now expected to bring death to the bull. In both cases, death, like the preceding swordplay, had to be met with style. Even the act of dying was made part of the performance. As Koestler wrote about his Capuan gladiator-school owner: 'He has succeeded in impressing on his men as a golden rule that, once beaten, they should never ask to be spared, should cut a good figure whilst being finished off, and not disgust the audience with any sort of fuss. "Anyone can live, but dying is an art", he kept admonishing his gladiators.'

For audience and combatants alike this was of great importance, for it allowed death to be formalized and to be made the simple outcome of a game. Death in the arena could appear as something different from death in the real world outside. Instead of the groans and all the usual show of dying, it could become a tight-lipped act performed to rules that everybody knew. No fuss, as Koestler said, that might disgust the audience; and for the gladiators the act of killing a comrade need not rouse guilt or any real horror. The arena has a curious power to set its own standards. We would be horrified to see one man smash another insensible in the street, yet we applaud a knock-out in a boxing match. In the same way, these stylized deaths must have possessed a theatrical unreality, which was deliberately enhanced by those slaves in devil's uniform who dragged away the corpses. These were not ordinary men who suffered – but gladiators. Death was their business. Cicero even advised his fellow-Romans to go to the arena to teach themselves the knack of dying well and a true Roman contempt for death – 'even these slaves with nothing in the world can show us all how men should die'.

Another way in which the gladiatorial games were slowly transformed into a spectator sport was through the emergence of a clear star-system among the gladiators. To some extent this was inevitable. The arena was a world in which survival depended strictly on success and as the shows tended to become regular events, they must have made a string of champions. In this sort of fighting, strength and experience counted. With each successful fight a man increased his chances of survival. At the top there were the true professionals, men of immense physique and skill who had mastered the art of killing as adroitly as a famous ball-player perfects his strokes.

We know such men survived. There was the charioteer-gladiator who had lived long enough to father the two sons who appealed for his freedom to the Emperor Claudius during a show. And throughout the Empire there are grave-inscriptions similar to the memorial to the gladiator, Publius Ostorius, at Pompeii, which records his fifty-one victories in the arena and the fact that, after winning freedom by his sword, he had still fought as a volunteer. These were the sort of men the young Tiberius paid a thousand gold pieces each to break their retirement and fight in his show.

Against such formidable old hands the chances of an untried

novice were extremely slim, and it is clear that in the arena there were two separate classes – the winners and their victims.

The victims were the men without much chance – newcomers, barely trained captives, men who had reached the limits of their skill. Only by luck or extraordinary skill and strength would they survive. It was different for the proven men. They would go into battle knowing the odds were firmly on their side.

The whole star-system was applied to them, and it would be wrong to class them with the captive victims lower in the gladiatorial scale. Whether theoretically free or not, these champions were primarily professional performers. In the arena they were governed by their oath. Outside it they were free to marry, have scandalous affairs, or, as we know again from Pompeii, live it up in the local brothel. These were the famous names, often fighting under some warlike *nom de guerre* like 'Hercules' or 'Pertinax' or 'Victor'. They could make fortunes from the prize-money of their victories, while their presence at the shows would guarantee the sort of action that the audiences loved.

Again, their skill had much in common with the modern matador's. The star would have his following of fans, who would bet on him, cheer for him, and follow each move he made in dispatching his opponent. From grave-inscriptions we know that star gladiators frequently retired to become free and wealthy members of society. Perhaps the most striking evidence of the status these gladiator-heroes could achieve under the Empire is to be found in the mosaic portraits of them that have survived. In the Lateran Museum and the enormous floor of the Villa Borghese in Rome, one can see the way rich Romans would even decorate their homes with pictures of them.

Dacian prisoner, as depicted on the Arch of Diocletian. Men like these provided the raw material for the arena.

These were the mosaics that Aldous Huxley said were 'full of the quintessence of the Roman reality'. No one, he said, should claim that he understood the Roman Empire without studying them. 'After looking at these mosaics a man can have no more generous illusions about the people who admired it or the age in which it was made. He will realise that Roman civilisation was not just as sordid as ours, but if anything more sordid.'

The final stage of the gradual transformation of the gladiatorial games into a modern-style spectator sport came when free men began to seek their fame and fortune alongside the unfree gladiators. Quite how and when this happened is not known. There always had been the opportunity for unfree star gladiators to stay on as 'volunteers' after they had earned the *rudius*. But the first explicit reference to volunteers entering the arena comes with those two violent swordsmen – the barrister-knight and the former senator – whom Caesar paid to fight to the death at one of his vote-catching rallies in Rome. Under the Empire volunteers became quite common – Livy distinguished two separate sorts of gladiators, 'slaves and free men who sell their blood'.

These volunteers fell into several categories and the audiences seem to have appreciated them more than slaves. The firmest favourites were the men of noble birth. Within this class-ridden, precedence-obsessed society, there was a particular pleasure in observing the highest in the land paying an audience the compliment of fighting for them. There was a double element in this. Even in modern Europe, aristocratic sportsmen have invariably been popular with the people – one thinks of princely cricketers like Pataudi, racing-drivers like Bira, Obolensky, who played rugger, while with Edward, Prince of Wales, people were always thrilled at his success as a competitor in point-to-point horse-races. But in Rome there was also a touch of envy in the way people enjoyed watching some aristocrat degrade himself by fighting among slaves.

As we have seen, this could become a matter of contention for the government. Nero and Commodus encouraged it as a way of showing their contempt for the aristocracy. So did Caesar. According to Friedländer, 'Caesarism, with its hatred of the aristocracy, its class levelling and favouring of the populace, would not regret the degradation of the upper classes; and the mob would be delighted at seeing the noblest in the state exhibit themselves like slaves and hirelings to provide a holiday.'

On the other hand, emperors concerned with public order or the maintenance of the *status quo* tried to forbid these noble gladiators. According to Tacitus, even Vitellius, the gluttonous ex-charioteer who ruled for ninety days before Vespasian, saw it as such a scandal that 'a severe warning was issued against Roman knights degrading themselves by gladiatorial fighting'. As we have seen, Augustus and Tiberius also did their best to stop the practice, but the popular demand was so insistent that there was always good money for any nobleman willing to risk his neck in the arena. Tacitus says that 'numbers of country towns in Italy competed by offering high sums to entice really degraded young men' into the arena as gladiators. Juvenal, that most irascible of snobs, got most indignant when a descendant of the great Gracchus enrolled as a *retiarius*, while in the reign of Marcus Aurelius there is the report of a notorious senator who

Women were the greatest novelty. Here a detail from a relief at Halicarnassus shows them fighting as gladiators in the arena.

blatantly assured the Emperor that he could see many praetors round him in the court who had at some time fought beside him in the amphitheatre.

The entry of these noble fighters into the arena was yet a further step towards turning the gladiatorial games into a sport. These gilded swordsmen were not strictly members of a gladiatorial school – although they would often train and receive instruction there. Nor would they necessarily be expected to do battle to the death. Their appearances would be more in the nature of special guest performances sandwiched between the other fights.

So were the appearances of a still more memorable form of volunteer gladiator – the fighting women of the Empire. For the Romans these were the novelty of novelties. Juvenal was very rude about them – in one of his satires he described a female gladiator as she laid down her sword and armour to relieve herself. And in AD 200, after a rash of female contests in the ring, the Emperor Septimius Severus banned them completely throughout the Empire. But for a while these women fighters had been popular. Nero was particularly fond of them, and, to judge by a carving in the British Museum showing two female gladiators from Halicarnassus in Asia Minor, they must have fought with great intensity. Clearly, though, they were something of a novelty, which, like the acrobats and clowns,

A memorial to the sweetheart – 'Modest Ludia' – of a gladiator, probably English – 'Lucius the gladiator'.

would bring some light relief between the serious contests. Only when they were of noble birth was their behaviour thought scandalous.

The bulk of the volunteers who entered the arena of their own accord seem to have been social outcasts, desperate characters who looked on this as a last resort to make their fortune, or tough adventurers who had grown bored with the even tenor of the *pax romana*. Tertullian exclaimed at 'how many idle men contract themselves out to the sword for the love of combat', and indeed, by the middle years of the Empire, the arena had become the one remaining place where the aggressive Roman could indulge his taste for blood. The frontiers were settled, and it became the policy of the emperors to rely increasingly on foreigners and barbarian recruits for the legions. According to Professor Grant, when the Italians were finally excluded from the predominantly German Praetorian Guard by Septimius Severus, many of the redundant guardsmen joined the gladiator schools.

But a close scrutiny of the names of freemen-gladiators shows that the great majority came from the lowest social classes – from men who had been slaves themselves or who were sons of slaves. This in turn suggests the unromantic truth that the main motive of these battling volunteers was economic – that they were generally poor men who signed on with a gladiator school for money and regular meals.

Despite this, the stories that were told about these freemen-gladiators were quite different. The Romans liked to think of them as if they were of noble family and had seen better days. The myths about them were the equivalent of those Victorian tales of gentlemen highwaymen and ruined sons of viscounts who espoused a life of elevated crime. There were the stories of good-looking young men like the Scythian Sisinnes who, in Lucian's tale, tried to help a friend by signing on to fight a gladiator in Amastris for a flat fee of ten thousand drachmae. Another story told of the dutiful but penniless young man who signed on in the arena to earn the money for his father's funeral. The Romans had a tendency to sentimentalize brutality.

(*Opposite*) with the disbanding of the Praetorian Guard, shown here during the period of the Emperor Hadrian, many of the guardsmen sought their fortune in the arena.

Coin from the Republican period, evidence that combats with wild animals appeared early in Roman history.

# VII The Beasts

During the 1850s, the energetic French who ruled the city at the time upset the Romans and the romantic foreigners in Rome by clearing the arena of the Colosseum of the rich jungle of greenery that had been growing there for centuries and starting to excavate. Nobody knew quite what they would find, but it was generally thought scandalous to strip the Colosseum in this way. Only a year or two before, an English botanist had spent many happy hours identifying and listing over a hundred separate varieties of plant life in this small area. Some of them were rare; some even came from Africa and Asia and were not normally found in Italy at all. His theory was that they were the descendants of plants seeded there directly from the feeds brought for the African and Asian animals in the arena.

It seemed a far-fetched theory at the time, but it was re-inforced by the discoveries of the determined Frenchmen. As they went ahead, their spades laid bare for the first time in centuries the centre of the Colosseum as it is today. The maze of walls and passages and cells under the arena revealed the ingenuity of this huge machine. Some of these subterranean areas had clearly been used for the scenery that contemporary accounts described rising up from the arena during the shows. Other parts housed the gladiators as they waited for their moment in the arena. But by far the largest part of this whole Colosseum underworld was used for animals. Careful detective-work was to reveal the ingenious arrangements that were made to produce these wild beasts in enormous numbers when they were needed on the floor of the arena. There were the dens, the ramps and even evidence of a large lift, worked with counterweights and pulleys, which carried the largest animals up to the arena.

The cellars beneath the arena were used to store the scenery and accommodate the beasts.

Mosaic showing a slave with a fully grown African lion – the Romans achieved great feats of animal-training.

These discoveries seemed to contradict contemporary accounts of the Colosseum. As we have seen, Suetonius' report of the inaugural games described in detail how the arena had been filled with water for aquatic games and battles. This would have been impossible without flooding the cellars, and it is now thought that these underground works were added at the end of the second century, when the Colosseum was being reconstructed after the fire damage of AD 192. They must have changed the character of the shows. Nautical performances were no longer possible. Instead, the Colosseum must have been increasingly devoted to the great spectacles involving wild animals on a scale the world has never seen before or since – the *venationes*.

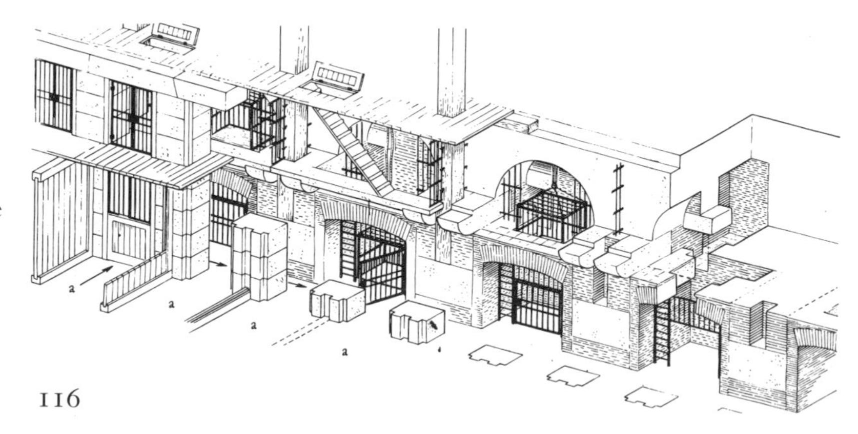


Diagram showing the working of the animal lifts installed in the Colosseum. The animals were driven into cages from the entries marked (a) and then hoisted to the floor directly below the arena. From here they were driven up a gangway and into the arena through a hatch.

Although held in the same arena and often on the same programme as the gladiatorial shows, these *venationes* were quite separate from them. They had a different origin, a different purpose and were conducted, not by gladiators, but by specially trained hunters called *bestiarii*. The *bestiarii* were generally looked down on by the gladiators and had their own training schools. In the arena they wore none of the splendid uniforms of the gladiators, nor did they practise anything approaching the gladiators' swordplay or style of fighting. They wore a belt, a simple linen tunic and fought with a sharp long-bladed animal spear – the *venabulum*. Generally they had no chance of becoming darlings of the crowd like charioteers or gladiators. One of the very few who did was the young Carpophorus, described by Martial as killing twenty beasts including lion, boar and bison in a single show of Domitian's in the Colosseum. It must have been a hideously dangerous trade. Lacking the glamour of the gladiators, it attracted few freemen volunteers although, according to Tertullian, *bestiarii* prided themselves upon their scars and bites as beauty-marks.

*Bestiarii* (specially trained animal-hunters) were quite distinct from true gladiators. Here they are represented fighting beasts in the arena.

Ulpian mentions unpaid volunteers who fought the beasts of the arena out of sheer bravado. Such men were exceptional. Most *bestiarii* were slaves, their death-rate high, and some of their feats of wholesale slaughter of wild animals recorded by the historians of the time are all but incredible.

More even than the gladiatorial games, these massive hunting shows were the direct expression of Rome's imperial ambitions and world-wide power. The Romans always had been dedicated hunters, and from the early Republic there are accounts of hunting rites of great antiquity. These continued through to the Empire. During Augustus' reign the festival of Ceres was still being celebrated by turning foxes loose in the Circus Maximus with firebrands tied to their tails. During the festival of Flora, hares and goats were publicly hunted in the Circus.

But it was not until Rome started to expand and conquer lands beyond Italy that its citizens so much as saw an exotic animal. They came to Rome as warlike booty.

The first time Rome saw elephants was in the triumph of Curius in 275 BC after the defeat of the Greek armies of Pyrrhus at Beneventum. Ever since Alexander's Eastern conquests, the Greeks had known of elephants. Pyrrhus had used them with his cohorts against the legions to produce a tactical surprise. This had not worked. The Roman legions were always able to cope with these tanks of the ancient world, and Rome never made much use of the elephant for warlike purposes.

Instead, from the beginning, elephants were creatures of wonder and display for the Romans, who called Pyrrhus' four Indian elephants 'Lucanian Cows', after the part of Italy where they had first appeared. Nobody knows what became of them, but they had set a fashion. Twenty-five years later, when Lucius Metellus beat the Carthaginians in his great victory at Palermo, he once again brought back captured elephants to Rome to take part in his triumph and boost his personal prestige. There were a hundred of them, African elephants this time, and bigger than Pyrrhus' four Indian ones. Metellus got them safely across the Straits to Reggio, supposedly on a huge raft built on barrels. Their mahouts were with them, and the elephants made an impressive entry into Rome, finally parading in a massed display in the Circus.

Again, there is no record of the fate of this herd of elephants, but a tradition was established which Rome never lost. The wild animals of Africa and Asia could be legitimate spoils of victory. They would delight and overawe the crowd, reflecting glory on the great men who provided them. They were the playthings of the people, who regarded them with the amazement and destructiveness of children given some precious object they can never understand.

This explains what always saddens naturalists about the Romans' almost total unconcern for this unrivalled offering of the world's most splendid creatures. There was no curiosity or feeling for them – except for how they could be used for maximum display. Apart from a few private animal collections, there was no interest in a zoo in Rome, although the Egyptians and the Persians had both built up zoos where wild animals were bred and studied in captivity. Instead, the Romans greedily consumed every animal that their conquering generals could bring back to Rome. They gaped at them, were frightened of them, and accordingly destroyed them.

Rome scoured the world to bring animals to the games. This slave is driving an ostrich on to a ship for a journey that would probably end in the arena.

Just after the Second Punic War *africanae bestiae* were imported to be hunted and destroyed in the Roman shows. By the second century BC the *venationes* had begun in earnest. By then Rome was becoming the dominating power in North Africa and Asia Minor. Carthage was destroyed and her lands made a Roman province in 146 BC. From then on these rich game lands were plundered to supply the arenas of the Roman world.

It did not take the Romans long to turn their ancient ceremonies of hunting hares and foxes in the Circus Maximus into a more impressive sort of sport. The same adaptive skills that had converted Etruscan funeral rites into the Roman gladiatorial show were soon developing popular spectacles of full-scale hunts involving wild beasts. Almost inevitably, animals were no sooner found and introduced to Rome than they were consigned to the arena. A new species must have seemed rather like a fresh style of gladiator. The *africanae bestiae* – the collective name is interesting in its imprecision – seem to have been lions and leopards, although it is likely that bears were also brought from North Africa at this time. So were ostriches. These were set loose – exactly like the wretched hares in the festival of Flora – and hunted across the Circus Maximus.

The Romans evidently enjoyed destroying these big defenceless birds. The Emperor Commodus finally won the all-time record as an ostrich-hunter. Using arrows with crescent-shaped tips and firing from the imperial box, he decapitated a hundred at a single session in the Colosseum. According to Dio Cassius, he then held a severed ostrich head towards his courtiers, and leeringly implied that they would soon be meeting the same fate if they weren't careful.

The death-rate of imported animals had not reached quite this level under the Republic, although the custom for rich men to canvass votes with lavish *venationes* was firmly established by the first century BC. By the year 169, Livy had noted that the curule aediles gave a show in the Circus Maximus in which sixty-three African beasts, including elephants and bears, were hunted. Soon afterwards the Senate passed a decree forbidding the import of *africanae bestiae* to Italy – presumably to check the undue influence of the shows on the people. This was quite ineffective; the importation and the shows continued.

These unknown animals of Africa and Asia were important counters in the prestige game of Roman politics. Ferocious beasts held an extraordinary symbolic power for the Romans and were ideal for impressing the unsophisticated, bloodthirsty mob – a perfect way of flattering them and bringing home to their imaginations something of the foreign conquests of Roman arms. At the same time, for the ambitious generals, plutocrats and politicians, the arena came to be a rough-and-ready index of the power they wielded. They could find animals for it in several ways, all of them related to the possession of great power or influence. Wild beasts could be bought – but at such vast expense that this required a fortune. They could be obtained through influence or pressure on the new territories of Africa or Asia. Or they could be won by victory and brought back directly by Roman conquerors wanting political power in Rome. During this period of the Republic all three methods were extensively employed. The result was an influx of new and rare animals for the arena on a scale the world has never seen before or since.

Lion and hippopotamus depicted on coins of the Emperor Philip the Arab minted to commemorate the games held in the Colosseum as part of the celebrations of the thousandth anniversary of Rome's foundation.

The plutocrats produced the most tasteless and unpleasant sights of all, such as the full-scale elephant fights staged in the Circus Maximus by Claudius Pulcher during his aedileship in 99 BC. A few years later his successors as aedile, Lucius and Marcus Lucullus, tried to go one better by arranging fights between elephants and bulls. Rome's first fight of 'a number of lions together', as Pliny called it, came about 95 BC, and was paid for by the consul, Mucius Scaevola.

It was another wealthy politician, Marcus Scaurus (who built the first amphitheatre in Rome), who also brought the first hippopotami and crocodiles to the city. In this case his animals represented both wealth and foreign influence. To capture and bring a hippopotamus from Egypt must have been an enormous undertaking. (In 1850 an entire army division was required to capture the first hippopotamus that was brought to

Trade in animals for Rome's arenas reached vast proportions. This mosaic shows tiger, antelope and bison being dragged to a ship bound for Rome and (*left*) the capture of a rhinoceros.

Europe since Roman times. It travelled from Alexandria to London in a steamer with a specially constructed freshwater tank, along with two cows and ten goats to supply its milk requirements.) But Scaurus had also been governor of Syria and it is likely that the 150 leopards that he turned loose in his new arena had been brought from there.

As Friedländer points out, 'Roman grandees generally owned land in Africa and Asia and could utilize the friendship of provincial governors and thus expedite the importation of animals.' When Cicero was provincial procurator in Cilicia in 51 BC, the aedile, Marcus Caelius, wrote to him asking for more panthers to be sent to Rome for his forthcoming show. The ten he had already sent were not enough. 'He need only issue the commission; food and transport have already been provided.' Friedlander comments on this letter that 'as a return favour was extremely probable, such requests were not lightly refused'.

But in providing beasts for the arena, no politician or mere millionaire could hope to equal the great Roman generals. They could bring back the beasts of Africa and Asia as booty or as tribute, and it was thanks to them that the *venationes* reached a peak of extravagance during the last years of the Republic. When Sulla turned his ambitions from the battlefield to Roman politics, he set the pattern for the shows to come. His praetorship was celebrated with a hunting display of a hundred maned lions let loose and killed in the Circus Maximus. The lions were the gift of his friend and ally, Bocchus, King of Mauretania.

Embarking an antelope for Rome.

A *bestiarius* fighting a leopard. Detail from a mosaic in the Villa Borghese.

So were the hunters – skilled Mauretanian spearmen who had learned to deal with lions in the wild. This was a unique performance – according to Seneca the first time lion had been freely hunted in this way on such a scale – and must have done more to establish Sulla's reputation with the populace than all his victories. It also paved the way for the climax of the Roman animal shows during the battle for supreme power between Pompey and Caesar.

It was a bizarre affair – a period of madness and vulgarity as these two masters of the world attempted to daze their enemies and flabbergast the Roman people into granting them the power they wanted. It provides one of history's supreme examples of what the economist Thorstein Veblen described as the process of 'conspicuous waste': the attempt to gain prestige through profligacy, to demonstrate one's wealth and power by squandering it. As Veblen pointed out, this seems to be a basic concomitant of power. Tribal chieftains, medieval kings and modern corporations rarely seem entirely immune to it. Sometimes, as with the eighteenth-century European aristocracy or the twentieth-century military state, conspicuous waste becomes contagious and ultimately self-destructive. But nowhere has this strange phenomenon appeared in quite the form it did during this period in Rome.

By the year 55 BC, Pompey had won power and influence such as no Roman had enjoyed before. He was the conqueror of Africa and Asia Minor. Numidia was ruled by his nominee, King Juba, while in the East his armies had won Syria, Armenia, Pontus and had reached the Caucasian frontiers. In Egypt his influence had just restored Ptolemy Auletes to the throne. Syria was governed by his man, Gabinius. All that now remained to be won was Rome. As part of his struggle against the aristocratic party he had already built a temple to Venus Genetrix and a vast theatre – Caesar was to be murdered there, and its site can still be seen off the Corso Emmanuele. To celebrate the opening of the theatre and the dedication of the temple, he staged his games, which were intended as the ultimate demonstration of his greatness.

They turned out to be more revealing than he intended. For along with his wealth and world-wide influence, so amply represented by the menageries of rare beasts he poured so recklessly into the arena, came something else – the first hint of his limits as a man and as a politician. No one could deny that he was doing more than any rival of the time could manage; according to Pliny the animals included 600 lions (315 of them with manes), 410 *variae* (leopards and other large cats), a Gallic lynx which Pliny called a *chama* and described as having a wolf's shape and a leopard's spots, and a rhinoceros. Pliny specifically describes this as the one-horned variety, so that it must have been an Indian one, which would have reached Rome overland by way of Egypt. Pompey also showed a troupe of monkeys, thought to have been brought from Alexandria.

The climax of the show was planned to consist of twenty elephants brought specially from Africa. According to one account, their drivers had promised the animals, when inducing them aboard their ships, that they would not be hurt. The promise was not kept, and on the last day, when they were paraded in the Circus Gaetulian huntsmen from North Africa started to massacre them. Much as the Roman people loved to witness bloodshed in the arena, there was something in the destruction of these huge animals that disgusted them. One animal roused the admiration of the crowd by continuing to fight when beaten to its knees and snatching at the huntsmen's shields until they lay round it in a circle. Another was killed by

Two mosaics from Nennig, Germany, showing (*left*) a *bestiarius* with a wounded leopard and (*right*) a bear trampling on a *bestiarius*.

a direct hit with a javelin below the eye. Some of them tried to break out through the iron bars that penned them in, while their agony and trumpetings were so pitiful that the 'spectators rose and cursed Pompey for his cruelty'. According to Dio Cassius, Pompey was forced to call off the slaughter, although he had the survivors killed later. Cicero wrote to a friend that the people in the Circus not only pitied the elephants, 'but also felt that the elephant was somehow allied with man'.

One feels that with a people as bloodthirsty as the Romans, Pompey must have handled things extremely badly to allow the climax of his games to end in such disaster. When his rival, Caesar, employed the same techniques to bid for popularity, he used more finesse and showed that he possessed what Pompey evidently lacked – a flair for mass psychology and a genius for showmanship. When he had elephants fighting for him in the Circus Maximus, no one objected. They were used, twenty a side, along with cavalry and infantry, for a full-scale battle. Instead of simply throwing animals into the arena to be slaughtered, he built up splendour and excitement. Leopard-fights had grown familiar by now. Instead of using them again, Caesar introduced the novelty of Thessalian bullfighting into Rome. Pliny described the excitement of the scene when the Thessalian horsemen galloped alongside the bull, seized it by its horns, and with a sudden twist broke its neck.

As we have seen, Caesar also knew how to use exotic animals to enhance his personal prestige. Antony had evidently shocked the Romans when he drove out with the notorious actress, Cytheris, in a fine chariot drawn by lions. Caesar, in contrast, seems to have roused the people's admiration with the forty torch-bearing elephants he had lighting his way up to the Capitol during his quadruple triumph in 46 BC. He also managed to produce a final wonder to amaze the people – the first giraffe exhibited in Rome. This had probably been brought from Alexandria.

With the death of Caesar and the beginning of the Empire under Augustus, the pattern of the great *venationes* changes. In place of those ambitious politicians unloading the animals of Africa into the arena in egomaniac extravaganza, there is now the state. The shows go on. The taste for them is now so solidly engrained that the people would feel cheated without them. And as with gladiators, dangerous animals can play their part in enhancing the imperial mystique. But the air of competition, which had made rival generals and contending millionaires use wild beasts in their battles for power, is past. Instead, the Emperor turns the *venationes* in Rome into a state monopoly. The slaughter and supply is likewise regularized. As Friedländer writes in one of his most colourful passages: 'For one great Roman festival, with due Roman splendour, the Hindu tamed elephants to catch elephants, the Rhinelanders spread nets over the boars in the reeds, Moors on their hardy ponies encircled ostriches in the deserts and lurked in the horrible solitudes of the Atlas by the lion-pits.'

Under the Empire, the demand for animals actually increased. Augustus claimed to have given the Roman people ten thousand wild beasts in *venationes* during his reign; if Suetonius was accurate, Titus had five thousand slaughtered in a single day at the opening of the Colosseum. With the Colosseum functioning, the demand continued. By now it could hardly be satisfied by the spoils of battle or by those gentlemanly arrangements with provincial governors which had supplied the wild beasts for Rome under the Republic. The supply of animals became an industry.

Once more one must admire the effectiveness of Rome's administration and its business methods. Even today wild animals are notoriously hard to catch and transport for long distances. But in a world devoid of high-speed transport and the sophisticated methods of the modern hunter, the arenas of the Roman world were kept supplied for more than three hundred years with live beasts of every shape and size from every corner of the known world. Nothing approaching this enforced migration of wild animals has ever happened since. Before it ended it had permanently cleared North Africa and parts of Asia Minor of the large game animals that previously existed there in large numbers. Thanks to the continuing demands of the arena, a whole area was now made safe for large-scale cultivation. As with the British settlers in nineteenth-century Africa, the colonist and hunter advanced hand in hand.

Much of the incentive for this widespread and methodical hunting came as usual from the imperial government. In Rome an official procurator was in charge of the supply of beasts for the emperor's shows; he and his department must have combed the Empire and beyond for animals. There is a tantalizing dearth of knowledge of their activities. It is known that they were helped by certain laws, such as the decree which placed an obligation on all towns within the Empire to provide food and transport for beasts travelling to Rome for the Emperor's games. There was also an imperial edict which made elephants the Emperor's beasts – no private individual could own or kill them. At the port of Ostia there were special cages, owned by the Emperor, where beasts were unloaded from the ships, before they made the final journey into Rome.

But it is clear that the continual demand for beasts for the arena created an established trade in animals throughout the Empire. The so-called 'Hunting Baths', miraculously preserved in the sand-dunes outside the Tripolitanian settlement of Leptis Magna, give just a glimpse of how this trade was organized. The 'Baths' are strongly built with a central barrel-vaulted hall and stone outbuildings. A fresco on the main wall gives an impressive picture of Roman hunters fighting leopards in the arena. Whoever built the place was evidently prosperous; Mortimer Wheeler's theory is that it was 'the property of a guild of hunters whose trade was to supply wild beasts to local Italian amphitheatres'. From Tripoli it would have been no problem to sail animals to Ostia, and it is certain that there were other hunting guilds like this along the whole of the North African coast. The hinterland had been a great game area at the beginning of the Empire and it continued to supply *africanae bestiae* to Rome at least until the reign of Constantine. But with the settlement of the North African cornlands, hunters must have had to travel further south for their quarry, and there is evidence that, from the first century onwards, the supply of wild beasts from the north of Africa had begun to dwindle.

The effect of this was to compel the Roman animal merchants and the civil servants catering for the arena to look around for different animals from fresh sources. A further influx of still stranger animals started to arrive in Rome. Tigers from India

Victim of the arena – a criminal *condemnatio ad bestiam.*

and northern Persia became quite a common sight in the arena. So did bears from Asia Minor. By Trajan's reign camels, several kinds of antelope, wild asses, elk and bison had all appeared in the arena of the Colosseum. There were also some mysterious rarities which naturalists still argue over. Some believe that the white bear Pliny ascribed to Nero was in fact a polar bear. This is quite possible; by this time Roman trade was penetrating to the far North, and any strange beast was known by now to be valuable. Jennison's authoritative opinion is however that 'it is more likely to have been an albino of the straw-coloured bear of Syria or "white" bear of Thrace'. There were also panthers, cheetahs, lynxes, more giraffes and the most startling rarity of all – a Siamese white elephant which is said to have appeared in one of Trajan's triumphs.

Until the last days of the Empire the arena of the Colosseum occasionally became the scene of a ritual holocaust of animals. The Emperor Trajan had over ten thousand animals slaughtered there during the four months of his celebrations for his Dacian triumph, and the Roman people never lost their taste for serial slaughter of these menageries of rare, uncomprehending beasts. For a great celebration, such as the rejoicing for the millenary of Rome under the Emperor Philip the Arab in AD 248, nothing sufficed except to turn the sand of the arena scarlet with their blood. But at the same time there were other uses for the animals in the arena.

One was to employ them as an exciting and original means of execution. The Romans' ancient enemies, the Carthaginians, had been the first to throw their military deserters to be trampled underfoot by elephants. The Romans found this an idea to emulate; before long they had introduced the punishment, *condemnatio ad bestiam,* as an approved way of dealing with serious criminals. Under the disordered late Republic, this might arguably have been adopted as an emergency deterrent to strike terror into Rome's most dangerous criminals. Under the Empire, it had ceased to enjoy even this justification. *Condemnatio ad bestiam* had become both arbitrary and erratic. Under such potentates as Nero and Caligula it increased, and generally appears to have been less of a legal penalty than one further means of titillating the sadistic instincts of the mob. Under these emperors there were scenes of mass executions in the arena, with malefactors tied to posts and ripped apart by hungry carnivores. This must have been inefficient as well as horrifying. There are no carnivores which will willingly eat human flesh in the wild; in the arena the animals were often goaded on with fire or hunger, but even then they would often leave the victims mutilated and visibly alive. Animals were also used in the sort of tableau that was popular throughout the Empire. In one of these a criminal was made to appear to fly, only to fall among a group of lion in the arena. During Domitian's reign a good-looking criminal was dressed to play the part of Orpheus. At the conclusion of his act he was devoured by a Caledonian bear.

Condemned man being savaged by a leopard.

To offset scenes like these, one must remember that the animal shows of the arena also relied increasingly upon the expertise of animals and their trainers. An audience might actually prefer a trick to a kill. It is not only the bullfight that finds its origins in the arena with Caesar's Thessalians. Many of the traditions of the modern circus can be traced directly back to the animal acts performed in the Colosseum and the arenas of the Empire as light relief during the Emperor's spectacles. There are examples of animal-training from antiquity – Greek temples often kept a tamed lion, and the trainers of Alexandria were celebrated during Republican times. But it was during the first and second centuries AD in the Roman shows that the art reached its highest level. Pliny described the bulls he saw in the arena which fought, rolled over, and let themselves be caught by the horns at their trainer's word of command. Some of them even stood like charioteers in special chariots going at a gallop. Seneca, like most Romans, seems to have been fascinated by the feats of animal-trainers – he described one who put his hand into a lion's mouth, another who kissed his tiger, and a Negro dwarf who could order his elephant to walk the tightrope.

In the arena, performances by trained elephants, horses and even bulls trained to work in water (such as appeared at the inauguration of the Colosseum) seem to have been quite common. But the Roman taste was essentially bizarre. What thrilled the audience was to see animals trained in defiance of the laws of nature, lions which chased hares round the arena and then brought them back unharmed to the trainer, leopards which walked peacefully with antelopes, crocodiles which allowed Egyptian boys to ride them in the water and then walk unscathed among them. But it was the Emperor Elagabalus who carried this taste to extremes. In public he enjoyed driving a chariot harnessed to lions, tigers and even stags – notoriously the most difficult of all beasts to break to harness. In private this emperor had the habit of turning his tame lions, bears and leopards into the bedrooms of his drunken guests. The animals were so well trained that nobody was ever hurt.

(*Overleaf*) reconstruction of the Forum and Colosseum during the reign of Constantine I (306–37).

# VIII Hub of Empire

The Colosseum as it appears on a medallion of the Emperor Gordian III.

With the completion of the Colosseum it becomes obvious how this building rounded off Vespasian's concept of the restored, enhanced Augustan Empire. From now on the state's important function of participating in regular gladiatorial games and *venationes* would be concentrated here. The size and shape and the position of the Colosseum established it for what it was – the hub of Rome, the Empire in microcosm. It was to be much more than the place where the bored Roman masses were kept quiet with bloodthirsty shows. It was intended as the setting for what could now become the central ritual of the Roman state. The traditional observances of the Republic had grown archaic and largely meaningless. The state religion was a formalized affair, with little significance for the mass of citizens. Whatever popular political life Rome had known ended with the Empire.

Only within the shows was there a sign of corporate vitality. Only within the massed enthusiasm of the enormous audiences was there a unifying force able to link the disparate and disorderly populace of Rome into the semblance of an imperial people. Augustus had shown how to use this unifying force. True, it relied on bloodshed, games and massed spectator sports, but this was all his Empire had to offer in the way of mass emotional appeal. It had grown too fast to generate its own mystique or to bind its teeming citizens into any sort of imperial purpose. As we have seen, Augustus built his great imperial festivals out of the competitive vote-catching spectacles of Pompey, Caesar and the late Republic. Now Vespasian had brought this movement to its logical conclusion with the Colosseum. Here it could assume its finished form.

The Emperor Domitian sets out on a war expedition.

In its way, his building represents an original Roman contribution to the art of government. Under the Greeks an ideal had evolved of the state existing to provide for man's needs as a political animal. This ideal had changed, and in Vespasian's Rome this change was perfectly expressed within this massive, closed-in architectural form of the Colosseum.

The Roman Empire had created the world's first mass urban populace; from now on the Empire would exist to provide for the individual's needs as a spectator. The Greek ideal of the individual had been active – man was a political animal. But in the Roman Empire it was passive – man was a spectator. As a spectator he fulfilled himself, satisfied his needs beyond the mere provision of his livelihood and did his duty to the Emperor.

Every Roman city, however far from the centre of the Empire, had its gladiators. These are depicted on a mosaic found at Zliten in Tripoli.

Titus' hundred-day inaugural games in the Colosseum were of course exceptional. Not even first-century Rome could have continued to expend its men and animals on such a scale. And it was really under the reign of Titus' disloyal brother and successor, the imperial Domitian, that the Colosseum entered its stride and started playing a regular part in the Emperor's government. Titus' death had not interrupted work on the building. If anything, Domitian was more obsessional a builder than his father, repairing the Capitol, raising fresh temples to Jupiter and to his dynasty, and building a stadium, a forum, a concert hall, an artificial lake for sea battles. Somehow he also found the resources to add the fourth storey on to the Colosseum, and it is likely that the interior was virtually completed by the time he died.

Officially it was still named after his dynasty with the name Vespasian had given it – The Flavian Amphitheatre; and for Domitian the arena now became the centre of his popular cult, which he took far more seriously than Titus had. There were no great innovations in his shows or in their staging. For some reason he was unusually fond of watching women gladiators in the arena, so that the Colosseum must have seen these Amazonian gladiators early in its history. He was also so anxious to keep the action going that he had special lighting installed, including a massive iron chandelier. Whether Rome ever saw an all-night show is not recorded.

Like so many emperors before and after him, Domitian appears to have had a sadistic streak that was exacerbated by the unhealthy possibilities of absolute power. It is hard to tell whether the arena played the same part in his degeneration as it had with Nero and Caligula. But it seems more than likely that the impressive nature of the Colosseum, which was also something of a family shrine, prevented his sadistic instincts from getting out of hand in quite the way they did with these two other emperors. This was a solemn building that imposed its rituals even on the Emperor, and Domitian treated it with an exaggerated sense of dignity.

He founded a new gladiator school in Rome, and it was at his initiative that the city's four training schools became maintained and run exclusively by the state. He also started an imperial troupe of gladiators, consisting of the finest fighters in the Empire. These were the men the crowds adored. Their expertise rebounded to the credit of the Emperor. When they appeared within a show they would provide the climax to the whole performance, a treat the Emperor was offering his grateful people. Sometimes he graciously presented them in answer to the popular demand. Suetonius describes how he 'allowed the people to demand a combat between two pairs of gladiators from his own troupe, whom he would bring on last in their gorgeous livery'. At that moment the gladiators had reached their supreme position in the Empire; they had become great ceremonial figures of the state, entrusted with the honour and the popularity of the Emperor.

Unlike his avaricious father, Domitian spent wildly on his shows. He lacked Vespasian's money sense, and the expense of all his spectacles undoubtedly helped bring him to the state of near bankruptcy he had reached by the end of his reign. But for Domitian the crowd inside the Colosseum *was* the Roman people. These were his subjects, and by presiding at their shows he could reach them, rule them and win their support. Suetonius has written that when he took back his wife Domitia after her notorious affair with the actor Paris he was 'delighted to hear the audience in the Colosseum shout: "Long live our Lord and Lady".'

Although Domitian was quite happy to allow the audience to ask him for a duel between imperial gladiators, he could not allow this freedom to turn into disrespect. Indeed, it is interesting to compare his behaviour towards the Colosseum audience with that of his brother Titus. Good-natured Titus had been very easy-going at the shows. True, he was a keen fan of the Thracian gladiators, but this had never stopped him tolerating the crowd's banter when his favourite lost. Domitian was quite different. For him the games had now become inseparable from his dignity. This extended even to the gladiators he favoured. Since Titus had supported the 'lights', he was for the 'heavies'. They were his party. His honour and his self-respect were involved with them. To criticize the heavies was to criticize the Emperor. Suetonius has recorded that:

> A chance remark by one citizen, to the effect that a Thracian gladiator might be 'a match for his Gallic opponent but not for the Patron of the Games' was enough to have him dragged from his seat and – with a placard round his neck reading, 'A Thracian supporter who spoke evil of his Emperor' – torn to pieces by dogs in the arena.

Domitian died. His death, by one of those strange quirks of fate that seemed to rule Roman history, heralded the Golden Age of Rome, that period which was to inspire Gibbon's most effusive testimonial: 'If any man were called to fix the period in the history of the world during which the condition of the human race was most happy and prosperous, he would, without hesitation, name that which elapsed from the death of Domitian to the accession of Commodus.'

This was the period of eighty-four years which took in the reigns of Nerva, Trajan, Hadrian, the Antonines and ended with the death of the saintly Marcus Aurelius. It was also the period – and this Gibbon omits to say – when the Colosseum seemed to establish itself ever more insistently in both the life and the imagination of the Roman Empire. In Rome its popularity virtually destroyed the Greek athletic games: 'The crowd,' says Carcopino, 'addicted to the thrills of the Colosseum, looked on them as colourless and tame; and they enjoyed no greater favour among the upper classes who professed to detect an exotic degeneracy and immorality in their nudism.'

And not only in Rome: under Trajan the Senate actually forbade gymnastic games at Vienne in Gallia Narbonensis, and throughout the Empire provincial towns were building local versions of the Colosseum. The theatre suffered too. Now was the time when the sadistic tableaux involving criminals made their appearance in the Colosseum. Theatre audiences dwindled – in the next century the great Theatre of Marcellus in Rome was actually abandoned, while throughout Gaul and Macedonia, Professor Grant tells us, theatre architects were already busy 'modifying their building plans to accommodate gladiatorial duels and *venationes*'.

Can a period like this really be described 'without hesitation' as one of overwhelming human felicity? On the whole, later historians think not. For Mumford these first-century Romans, far from being happy, led a life in which 'attendance at public spectacles, terrestrial and nautical, human and animal, became the principal occupation of their existence', while in Rome, 'the usual activities of a city were subordinated to the mass production of violent sensations derived from lust, torture and murder'.

In his monumental study of Roman society, Samuel Dill came to the conclusion that there was a vein of 'coarse insensibility to suffering' running through the Roman character and that, if anything, this got worse under the Empire, largely because of the shows: 'From father to son, for nearly seven centuries, the Roman character became more and more indurated under the influence of licensed cruelty.' Even the great Stobart has to admit an element of doubt in his otherwise flattering account of first-century Rome when he mentions the Colosseum. This was, he believes, a period of great material advance. 'In such matters as transit, public health, police, water-supply, engineering, building and so forth, Rome left off pretty much where the reign of Queen Victoria was to resume.' But then he writes of the crowd in the Colosseum 'with the purple and gold awnings spread to protect them from the blazing sunshine, the auditorium perfumed with scents and cooled by fountains, and the arena at their feet flooded with water to present a naval combat. It is a city wrapped in profound peace, still dreaming amid its splendours that it is the mistress of the world.'

The truth was that Rome had grown increasingly addicted to the shows, and the building of the Colosseum had almost certainly made the addiction worse. The existence of this permanent great arena and the state-backed schools for gladiators and *bestiarii* guaranteed the continuity of the shows in Rome and provided an effective model for provincial towns to copy. With this, the popular demand had grown, making the arena a central part of Roman life.

The arena soon came to be one of the trade-marks of the Roman Empire. (*Left*) amphitheatres at Verona and Caerleon in Wales. (*Opposite*) at El Djem, in Tunisia, this copy of the Colosseum was made the centre of the Roman plan for the city.

(*Above*) the Emperor Marcus Aurelius (161–80), who attempted, quite unsuccessfully, to restrain the Roman taste for the arena. Trajan (180–92) (*below*) was more realistic, and gave the people what they wanted.

During this 'golden' period, three emperors made efforts to control or cut down on the shows. None succeeded. Trajan and Marcus Aurelius both attempted to extend the practice of *lusiones*, mimic battles not involving killing. Trajan provided *lusiones* during the thirty days of his festival in the Colosseum in March 108. But when he came to celebrate his Dacian triumph, he bowed to the peoples' wishes and provided them with gladiatorial shows of the old style. Marcus Aurelius went further. According to Carcopino, 'obeying the dictates of his Stoic philosophy, he exhausted his ingenuity in reducing the regulations and budgets of the *munera* and in this way lessened their importance, and wherever it fell to him to offer entertainment to the Roman *plebs*, he substituted simple *lusiones*.' This did little for his popularity, nor did it have the faintest effect on the habits of his subjects. If anything he increased their taste for bloodshed, and, with the sort of irony the Romans could appreciate, his wife not only fathered a son on him by a gladiator, but this son turned out to be the gladiator-emperor, Commodus.

The Emperor Hadrian also made efforts to control the shows, despite his own well-known 'dabbling' in gladiatorial combat as a youth. As we have seen, one move he made was to forbid the compulsory consignment of slaves to the arena. Rather like Tiberius, he also made himself unpopular by his failure to preside over the shows in Rome because of frequent absences abroad; and, like Tiberius, he seems to have objected to the people's right to put their wishes to him in the amphitheatre. On one occasion, Stewart Perowne recounts, he became annoyed at the way the audience was cheering on its favourite fighter.

The Emperor, instead of indulging them, turned to the herald, who always stood at his side, just as the trumpeter stands beside the *alguazile* in the bullring today, and said, 'Tell them to shut up.' The herald, saying to himself, 'Does he think he is Domitian?' tactfully forebore to call the audience to order so peremptorily (and so ineffectually). Instead, he held up his hands, as though he had some important announcement to make. Gradually the hubbub subsided. When the crowd was silent and attentive, he simply said, 'That is what the Emperor wanted.' Hadrian realised that the man had saved him from a gaffe and thanked him.

On another occasion Hadrian apparently refused to listen to the crowd's clamour for him to order the liberation of a slave chariot-driver who had won their hearts by his daring in the Circus. Rather than allow them to attempt to sway him, he ordered a herald to carry a placard on which was written coldly, 'You have no right to demand the freedom of a slave who is not your own property, nor to ask me to secure it for you.'

It was hardly surprising that Hadrian was not popular with the crowd, but, despite his dislike of these mass entertainments, he seems to have accepted their necessity and learned that they could not be changed. He also seems to have learned with time what was expected of him in his role as emperor. The words that Marguerite Yourcenar ascribes to him in old age in her remarkable book, *Memoirs of Hadrian*, are most convincing on this point.

Hadrian (117–38), another emperor who found himself forced to perpetuate the bloodshed in the Colosseum.

I learned to endure the games, where hitherto I had seen only stupid and brutal waste. My opinion had not changed; I detested these massacres where the beast had not one chance, but little by little I came to feel their ritual value, their effect of tragic purification on the ignorant multitude. I wanted my festivities to equal those of Trajan in splendour, though with more art and decorum. I forced myself to derive pleasure from the perfect fencing of the gladiators, but only on condition that no one should be compelled to practise this profession against his will. In the Circus I learned to parley with the crowd from the height of the tribune, speaking through heralds, and not impose silence upon the throngs save with deference (which they repaid me hundredfold); likewise never to accord them anything but what they had a right reasonably to expect, nor to refuse anything without explaining my refusal.

Whatever the reasons these emperors of Rome's Golden Age had for wishing to control the shows – reasons of cost, of taste, of ordinary humanity – their efforts were quite unavailing. Indeed, it seems as if this licensed bloodshed had become an unavoidable ingredient of the whole ordered, tranquil, prosperous civilization of the high Roman Empire.

One of the strangest things about the shows is that, even at this time, no one objected to them. Prosperity and ease of living during this period seem to have brought a softening of manners. The harshness of Caesar's day was ending. People were gentler, slaves better treated, living was easier. Yet, apart from Hadrian's law against compelling slaves to be gladiators, none of this changed the general attitude to the arena. Rather the reverse. And not only did the public's dependence on the shows increase, but there was still no word of protest from the intelligentsia or the philosophers of Rome. Nobody echoed the lone cry of Seneca's early in Nero's reign that in the arena 'man drank the blood of man'. It was almost as if the walls of the Colosseum had formed a sanctuary for the brutality and clash of arms now disappearing from the world outside.

Not that these walls were really adequate to contain the sadism of the arena for ever. As we have seen, under a Caligula or a Nero the cruelty could always overflow and menace the world outside. This was a constant risk. On the accession of Commodus it happened once again.

Commodus was gladiator-mad. His father was a saint; he was a sadist. And in his obsession with the arena he even managed to exceed the mania of a Caligula. Alone of all the emperors he fought professionally and with total dedication in the ring, drawing a million sesterces from the imperial gladiatorial fund for every day he fought, and making it quite plain that for all his duties and responsibilities, all that concerned him was his career as a swordsman. According to one eyewitness, the historian Dio Cassius, Commodus 'devoted most of his life to ease and to horses and to combats of wild beasts and men'.

In preference to the palace and the court, he liked to live in the gladiator school, the Ludus Maximus, where he had his own private quarters in the first hall, an honour he was entitled to as a *secutor* first class. When he entered the school he used to be announced by heralds.

Unlike Caligula, who was so thrilled to have stabbed a gladiator to death during a mere sparring-bout, Commodus was clearly a skilful fighter. During the reign of his indulgent father he fought 365 bouts in the arena; when he was emperor himself he carried the figure to beyond a thousand. 'Proud of his mastery of the difficult art of left-handed fighting, he killed the animals he encountered, and none of the gladiators matched against him ventured to win.'

Like Caligula, he soon carried his obsession beyond the arena into ordinary life. He loved to see himself as Hercules reincarnated. The god's lion-skin and club were carried everywhere before him as the symbol of his imperial power, and placed before him on a golden chair. At home, wrote Dio Cassius, he still loved fighting as a gladiator to entertain his guests. Inordinately vain, his chief concern was with showing off his skill. 'Commodus managed to kill a man now and then, and in making close passes with others, as if trying to clip off a bit of their hair, he sliced off the noses of some, the ears of others, and sundry features of still others.'

Once he attempted to arrange a tableau in the Colosseum to demonstrate his role, like Hercules', as a destroyer of monsters. To do this, Dio Cassius records: 'He got together all the men in the city who had lost their feet as the result of disease or some accident, and then, after fastening about their knees some like-

Bronze medallion depicting the Emperor Commodus as Hercules, his favourite role.

nesses of serpents' bodies, and giving them sponges to throw instead of stones, killed them with blows of a club, pretending that they were giants.'

Finally, the arena played the same part as it had with Nero and Caligula in totally deranging the young Emperor. During the last year of his life – he was then nearly thirty – he lost contact with reality, and lived entirely for the arena. For more than two weeks, he staged a full-scale festival of gladiatorial games and *venationes* in the Colosseum, of which he was the solitary star. This was when he shot his hundred ostriches from the imperial box. Clad in his robe of purple with gold spangles, he also shot down a hundred bears in the same way, then carried on slaughtering animals every morning and fighting as a gladiator in the afternoon. When he was satisfied with his performance, it was time for the regular gladiators. Dressed this time as Hermes, messenger of death, he would personally pair off the gladiators for their combats, and make sure their swords were sharp. No quarter was allowed. And in contrast with the *lusiones* which his father had staged here, large numbers of the men were killed.

Not surprisingly, even his courtiers were terrified of him. Dio Cassius describes how senators and ministers would anxiously applaud him, shouting out: 'Thou art lord and thou art first! Of all men most fortunate! Victor thou art! And victor thou shalt be! From everlasting, Amazonian, thou art victor!

Mainly, it seems, from motives of pure self-defence, these very courtiers finally arranged to have Commodus strangled in his bath by his current favourite, an athlete known as Narcissus.

Victory and defeat.

# IX The Game

The order Gibbon so admired had been the product of a static, universal state. Its framework had been set up by Augustus, and, despite the subsequent upheavals and a succession of disastrous rulers, this universal state had been steadily consolidated during the first century of the Empire. Political power became increasingly confined to an imperial bureaucracy and to a popular, presidential-style, military absolutism in Rome. The aristocracy lost their role as leaders which had been theirs under the Republic. They had no political or military function – nor had the people any. Rome's wealth was in the hands of a new class, the entrepreneurs and bankers who had made a killing on the opportunities of the Empire. Military power resided in professional armies who owed loyalty to the emperor who paid them. The whole rich area of the Empire had become a self-perpetuating system based on Rome – defended by its armies, administered by its bureaucrats, milked by its plutocrats and ruled by its emperors. This was the system which Vespasian repaired and then bequeathed to his successors.

This system had produced results which now seem ominously familiar – a great symbolic head of state, a large professional army in a time of peace, a moneyed class without political power intent on further self-enrichment, an aristocracy with snob-appeal and little else, and a great urban mass of people, grown largely parasitic on the wealthy and the state and in their turn dependent on a slave economy.

The vast material explosion of the Roman world had destroyed more than it created. Traditions and beliefs were rendered meaningless, religion became formalized and dead, the culture of a small aristocracy could hardly hope to keep pace with the mass society of Rome and the mixed cities of the

The Emperor Marcus Aurelius as he wished to be remembered by his subjects – distributing largesse. They would have preferred to see him applauding the games in the arena.

Empire. Behind the great buildings of the emperors lay a constant vacuum in a million minds.

This was the weak point of the Empire. The Roman world was neatly parcelled up among its proud possessors. But in the cities, and in particular in Rome, this strange new force in Roman politics, the unschooled, unrestrained mass of the people, had to be satisfied as well. If they were not, the Empire would collapse in chaos as it had nearly done during the anarchy of the 'Year of the Four Emperors'. To satisfy the people meant something more than simply to occupy their time, although naturally this did count. Just like today, Rome's basic industry was politics. This was what drew the money and the population to the crowded city, where an excess of wealth and shortage of employment meant that the majority existed in semi-idleness, supported by a tolerant employer, a patron of the state.

But as the programme of the state-provided games increased – until, as Carcopino reckons, half the total population of Rome could be seated simultaneously at a show – so the whole scope and purpose of the shows expanded. The construction of the Colosseum reveals the purpose of the static state; this was nothing less than to offer the multitude of Rome as spectators the functions they had long disclaimed as citizens. Here as spectators they were being presented the emotional equivalent of participating in something the Empire had long ceased to be – an expanding, open, social entity.

If, as the Greeks believed, man was a political animal, with certain urges that could be fulfilled only in politics, these needs were carefully observed and taken care of at the games. Indeed, at times the whole arrangement seems like a monstrous parody of popular politics. Cicero once wrote that there were three places where the people made their presence felt – in the popular assemblies, in the Roman *comitia*, and in the audiences at the games.

Thanks to the Empire, the first two institutions had been abolished, so that the third appeared additionally precious. According to Tacitus, the amphitheatre and circus were the people's 'temple, home and palace', where they showed least restraint before their rulers. 'In the utter lack of other occasions for public meetings and proclamations, the games gained additional significance', wrote Friedländer. In Republican times, politicians had paid great attention to their reception at the games and the theatre. And now 'the games afforded the emperors an opportunity of coming into personal contact and ingratiating themselves with the assembled people'.

Just as medieval English kings were said to have exercised supreme power 'in the presence of their people, lords and commons in Parliament assembled', so the emperors of Rome were at their most impressive when surrounded by their people at the games. In return, the people were accorded the unusual right of addressing the emperor as an equal. The episode when Commodus had one exceptionally tactless subject thrown to the dogs suggests that this was not a right to be abused – the degree of laxity varied from emperor to emperor – but in general the people were given the impression that they were participating with the emperor in an important act of state. Claudius always called the people at the games 'My Lords'. Titus 'used to satisfy every popular wish, take sides in the gladiatorial contests and, like one of the people, jeer at his opponents'. One of the reasons for the Emperor Hadrian's unpopularity was his dislike of acting on the wishes of the audience and liberating slaves who pleased them in the ring.

There were other ways as well in which the games were given the features of a genuine political assembly. One was the creation of supporters' clubs which could involve the engrained competitive loyalties of the people, just as political parties once had under the Republic. This reached its highest point not in the Colosseum, but in the circus with the blues, whites, reds and greens who supported their favourite charioteers. In Byzantium this process reached its culmination when the clash of circus factions led to political-style riots in the city. Rome avoided this, but in the Colosseum supporters of the 'lights' and 'heavies' hated their opponents and cheered on their champions with disturbing zeal.

Another basic political instinct is the need to choose some popular leader and then identify with him. This too was satisfied by the heroes of the ring and the arena – those Pertinaxes and Musclosuses did useful service in place of the popular leaders the Roman populace had lost.

And finally there was the audience's right of settling the life or death of a defeated gladiator. Professor Grant has told us that: 'The fallen fighter, if he was in a state to move, laid down his shield, and raised one finger of his left hand as a plea for mercy. The decision whether his life should be spared rested with the provider of the games; but he generally found it politic to take account of the spectators' loudly expressed views. Thumbs up, and a waving of handkerchiefs, meant that the man should be spared, thumbs down that he should not.'

This was of great importance, for it symbolized the principle

Relief from the Antonine Wall symbolizing the prosperity brought to the Empire by the *pax Romana*.

that here in the arena the Roman people still possessed supreme judicial power – the power of life and death. In delivering their judgment, the emperor was interpreting their will. Carcopino commented that 'here, and here alone, the people and the emperor could be one, united in the drama and the bloodshed of the fight, the awful ritual of the gladiator's death.' 'And here, in the Colosseum,' as Pliny wrote, 'the immense audience had the happiness of perceiving the *princeps* in the midst of his people, . . . sharing his emotions, his wishes, his pleasure and his fears.'

Just as the Colosseum was a substitute for politics, so it was also an effective surrogate for war. The frontiers of the Empire had been settled, the city walls pulled down, the battles fought. Even the legions now tended to be staffed with foreign mercenaries. Here, in this unnatural state of peace, the bold aggressive Roman could still actually observe, vicariously participate in, bloody battles.

War had been banished, but something of the emotional equivalent of war was being regularly waged throughout the Empire. Just as the emperor's presence and the people's power of life and death over a gladiator kept alive the political feelings of the multitude, so these combats to the death, safely walled in by the arena, efficiently indulged their warlike instincts.

As we have seen, the most dedicated fighting man who wanted bloodshed and adventure at first hand could enter the arena as a volunteer. Here, in this empire of universal peace, there was still a war to fight, an enemy to kill. Those praetorians who lost their job under Septimius Severus could continue their chosen *métier* here in the Colosseum. And the aggressive psychopath who felt the urge to kill could do so here.

But for the great mass of the spectators, the passive, non-participating members of a static state, the games also offered involvement in Rome's warlike past. These combats and these set-piece battles were nostalgic acts; soft city audiences were witnessing the equivalent of old war movies. Remember that the gladiators were all wearing the archaic uniforms of enemy troops from Rome's heroic period. The Empire was now wrapped in peace. The only real wars were occasional police affairs on distant frontiers waged by professionals who never entered Rome. Yet throughout the Empire gladiators were re-enacting the same bloodthirsty episodes – the cowboy stories of Rome's deeply cherished pioneering past. There were the *hoplomachi* from the wars with Sicily that had taken place two hundred years earlier, the *secutores* from the old campaigns in Thessaly, the charioteers from Britain, Rome's own Wild West.

And sometimes, as a special treat, the audiences were offered the supreme experience – the capture of a town, an infantry engagement from history, the naval battle waged in the dim past between Syracuse and Corinth.

This dream element was constantly recurring in the shows. We have already seen how the Colosseum was constructed as a sort of people's wonderland. With its gilded ceilings, scented fountains, and the continual fantasy of the scenery, the people were being offered their private portion of the wealth of Rome. This was the magic cornucopia of Empire. As well as a mass dream-substitute for politics and military adventure, the people were also being given a mirage of luxury.

For the Roman millionaire, wealth ultimately meant something not dissimilar from the furnishings and fantasies of the arena. Nero's Golden House seems to have been merely an overblown example of the way many a wealthy Roman lived, and the rich private houses and estates of the Empire often exhibited just the same theatrical excesses – landscaped gardens, herds of rare animals, buildings of exotic decoration, servants magnificently clad.

Here in the Colosseum – and on a lesser scale in the arenas throughout the Empire – much the same images of affluence were being proffered to the multitude. Nor were these offerings of wealth confined to visual fantasies. We have already seen how Domitian scattered his Numidian partridges among the Colosseum audience. Sometimes the offerings went further. On at least one occasion the entire audience at a show became the Emperor's guests. In Friedländer's words:

> At the December 1 festival in 88, according to Statius, the young and beautiful Imperial servants, in rich costume, waiting everywhere on the audience, fully equalled the spectators in number. Some brought costly dishes in baskets, and white napkins, and others, old wine. Children, women, plebs, knights and senate and the Emperor himself all dined at one board; and the poorest man could boast himself the Emperor's guest.

Much the same spirit lay behind the great imperial *venationes* staged in the Colosseum. Hunting was an imperial attribute. Some of the great game beasts were an imperial monopoly. The cost of hunting and bringing them to Rome was enormous, even for the emperor. And yet this lavish sacrifice of beasts and capital became an offering the emperor made to his people. It was a form of flattery, and with these week-long hunts staged for the people in the Colosseum, the emperor was inviting them to enjoy the very sport of emperors.

One of the prisoners of war who might have ended in the arena, depicted on a monument to Trajan's victories in Romania.

It can be no coincidence that the key developments in the Roman death-shows all came under the three main architects of the Empire – Caesar, Augustus and Vespasian. Each of these emperors built and adapted the existing drama of the arena into the popular ritual of the Empire. It is impossible to know how sophisticated their motives were, how much they planned the amphitheatre as the complex social instrument it finally became.

Probably not at all. All three rulers shared a pragmatic instinct for government, all of them had a practical ability to use what institutions were at hand; and in the way the shows developed there was the usual interplay of ruled and rulers, the emperors providing what the people wanted and in their turn ensuring that the needs of government were catered for.

If the Empire were to last, one of the central problems was urban order. Somehow the aggressive, active, undeferential populace of Rome had to be turned into the opposite – somehow the Empire had to make them non-aggressive, passive, deferential in the presence of authority. With quite uncanny skill, this was achieved largely through the shows. The citizens were made spectators, and gradually their discontents and aspirations could find their satisfaction only within the massive spectacles of Rome. (It is perhaps significant that the spectator disappears from history with the destruction of the Roman Empire, only to reappear in modern times.)

Before one totally condemns the Colosseum and all it stood for, one must in justice to the Romans be aware of just how much depended on it. It is hard to see what other institution at this point of history could have successfully united people and emperor as the Colosseum did. Killing is hideous in any context, and for a great empire to turn ritual killing into a central act of state is an obscenity.

But in the case of Rome, at least the killing was confined to the arena. Its savagery was kept in check by certain rules, and the whole system helped maintain a universal empire in which peace and order reigned for some five hundred years. The same cannot be said for the ever-increasing slaughter that went on in the disorder of the nation-states and warring empires that succeeded Rome.

In certain ways, the troupes of Roman gladiators and the whole organization that surrounded them can be compared with the rival armies which emerged in the later European nations. As was the case in these armies, the gladiators were in part maintained and trained and paid for by the state. They wore splendid uniforms, fostered a code of chivalry and dying, and had a strong sense of *esprit de corps.* To maintain them involved the state in something of a war economy, and their expense, their bearing and their warlike virtues enhanced the reputation of the rulers.

In other words, it seemed that in this peaceful static empire of the Romans gladiators performed certain of the functions later adopted by the rival armies of the modern world.

What was the difference between these gladiator armies of the Empire and national armies of today? Modern armies slaughter infinitely more and are more extravagant in their demands on national resources than the gladiators ever were. True, modern armies usually confine their killing to the soldiers, or more frequently to the citizens, of foreign nations, whereas the gladiators kept their killing to themselves. But the real difference, I suggest, is that in Rome this warfare was confined, controlled and turned into a game. Instead of causing devastation and upheavals, it was enjoyed and even made a source of unity and social order in the Empire. This substitute for warfare produced no massacres, no sieges in which towns were burned, no famine in which populations perished.

It is this element of warfare as a game enacted in the Colosseum which we inevitably find offensive. People enjoyed it, which is more than anyone can say for modern warfare – except possibly when watched a long way off on television.

But this tendency to conduct warfare by rule, and even play it like a game, is by no means confined to the Romans. As Johan Huizinga pointed out in his book, *Homo Ludens*, there is a long tradition of regarding warfare as a game, which can involve killing, but which is played according to strict rules. He wrote: 'The medieval tournament was always regarded as a sham-fight, hence as play, but in its earliest forms it is reasonably certain that the joustings were held in deadly earnest and fought out to the death.' He then instanced other examples ranging from the 'playing' of the young men before Abner and Joab in the Bible to such medieval and early Renaissance episodes as the Disfida di Barletta of 1503, 'where thirteen Italian knights met thirteen French knights' in deadly combat according to the strict rules of chivalry.

In essence, his whole thesis was that this game element in warfare, far from being actually distasteful, has in fact always proved a civilized and restraining force against the innate violence of society. A good example is the gentlemanly warfare waged by the *condottiere* armies of the Italian Renaissance – wars played out by well-known rules and carefully arranged to cause the minimum of suffering to society and to non-combatants. At the same time, traces of this 'play element' can be discerned, though with diminishing frequency, in European warfare until modern times.

By treating warfare in part at least as a game with certain rules, society could still try to control it. There were restraints. War still fell short of the wholesale murder of our modern total war. But the whole recent history of war shows a progressive weakening of these restraints. The American Civil War can be considered our first 'total' war. Since then, with the abandoning of any rules that interfere with victory, civilized man has finally lost control of war – with millions killed, societies destroyed and mass atrocities permitted.

Compared with this, how sane and civilized the controlled warfare of the Colosseum must appear. If warfare must occur – and history suggests it must – how skilful of the Romans to have devised such an effective substitute for it. At least their warfare, unlike ours, was kept under strict control, conducted with some style and strict rules, and rigorously confined to men who trained for it. Despite all later efforts at bringing the restraining 'play element' into warfare, only the slightly chilling genius of Rome went the whole way and made war entirely a spectator sport – something that could satisfy the aggressive instincts of great Empire, yet not disrupt its fate.

Huizinga quoted a psychologist's definition of a game as 'a representative act undertaken in view of the impossibility of staging real purposive action'. This was the essence of the games in the arena. In terms of politics, of social justice or of military aggression, these battles achieved nothing. That, for the Roman Empire, was their virtue. Had there been any *purpose* to the fighting, had the gladiators died for any reason beyond the game, their value would have gone. Had they fought real battles, they would have threatened the Empire, killed the innocent, shaken the reign of universal peace.

Instead the games served as an effective check to positive action, and to that instinct of aggression which would have wrecked the Empire.

The games in the arena were certainly the most powerful spectator sport ever devised by man. Our modern games seem pallid in comparison. The bull-ring madness, the mass absorption in international football, the whole religion of our modern games can never match the way society was drowned in these continuing spectacles. The drawing-power of the arena was clearly enormous. It was not simply for the rabble. All groups and classes found themselves drawn in, so that the games could come to form the central unifying mass activity of this enormous empire. They took the place of war, of social strife, of culture and of politics. Life was subordinated to them, and, by incorporating the imperial mystique with the shows, the emperors achieved the acquiescence of the multitude. Only the growth of Christianity came to rival them as a social force; and without them the peace and the cohesion of the Empire would have been impossible.

But there was a price to pay for this – something beyond the suffering of the thousands killed in the arenas and the undoubted coarsening of sensibilities. The ultimate effect of the games was to produce a sort of mass lobotomy among the populations of the Roman Empire. They were so powerful a force, so all-embracing, that they effectively displaced all popular initiative outside them. The part they played in the destruction of the theatre is generally accepted, although it seems the least of all the ills that followed. All feeling and all mass emotion drained to the arena, and then drained away. Through the games the people were so effectively diverted from reality that little else mattered. The substitutes had worked too well. The static world of Rome had gradually turned stagnant. People had lost all taste for war, for politics, for any mass emotion outside the circus or the arena. As their world crumbled they watched with total unconcern, sapped of all comprehension and ability to cope with what was destroying them. All that they had was the addictive dream of the arena. When the barbarians entered the city of Trier, they found the populace intent upon the games. The city had been undefended and the arena mattered more than the prestige of Rome or their own safety. It was the final nemesis.

Gladiatorial pop art. A Roman lamp in the shape of a gladiator's helmet – a pair of gladiators is even fighting on the crest.

# X Christian Victory

The first Christian emperor, Constantine the Great, whose uncertain voice ended the killing in the arena.

One of the great mysteries of the Colosseum is its relationship with Christianity. Today the ruin is officially a Christian shrine, restored and protected by a Pope, and made a centre of the cult of martyrs. And just as the conversion of the great cathedral church of Santa Sophia into a mosque after the fall of Constantinople symbolized the triumph of Mohammed, so this sanctification of the greatest monument of ancient Rome seems to represent the fall of paganism to Christ.

Much has been done across the years to emphasize this symbolism – the stark wooden cross erected on the spot of the emperors' podium, the Christian congregations that now take the place of the packed Roman audiences; and in his Easter pilgrimage and annual service at the Colosseum the Pope becomes as nowhere else the visible successor of the Caesars.

It is an impressive scene – this pagan building, the enthusiastic Romans, and, at the centre, one small figure whose authority still rivals the power of the ancient emperors. It would be hard to pick a more telling demonstration of Rome's continuity and of the way the Church became both victor and successor to the power of the Empire. And yet the truth behind this symbolism is elusive.

There is a tantalizing dearth of evidence – so much so that the Church itself is wary of claiming that a specific martyr definitely met his death here. A dedicated group of Roman Catholic scholars known as the Bollandists has made exhaustive studies of the Christian martyrs; but their leading scholar, the Belgian Delahaye, is sceptical as to whether actual martyrdoms occurred within the Colosseum.

The Colosseum, for Christians a shrine and place of martyrdom.

Others remain convinced that they did. During the seventeenth century, when the cult of Christian martyrs was in dramatic spate, the Colosseum was believed to have been an actual battlefield of the faith – the *luogo santo*, drenched with the holy blood of persecuted and dismembered Christians. This belief survives. As one quite recent historian, Edward Hutton, has written: 'It was upon the bloody floor of the Colosseum that Rome contrived her own slavery and our freedom. It was there that Christianity met the world and overcame it, there that the martyrs won for Christ his Kingdom in the hearts of men.'

One thing is undeniable: the profound Christian involvement in both the fate and myth of the Colosseum.

The slaughter in the Colosseum seen by an age of faith. Engraving by Jacques Blanchard (1600–38) of martyrs being thrown to the lions.

After that debatable 'Golden Age' of the Antonine emperors and the excesses of Commodus in the arena, the Colosseum's age of extravagance ended. The later Empire would produce no further Pompeys with their companies of elephants, no Tituses confident and rich enough to mount another spectacle that would last one hundred days. Nor would there be that air of wonder and surprise with which audiences had greeted Nero's fantastic scenery or Domitian's instant water-circuses. Rome's time of wonder was already over. The government had no surprises up its sleeve. Occasionally there were echoes of the massed combats and *venationes* of the past. In 248, the Emperor Philip the Arab matched several thousand fighting men – most of them barely trained prisoners-of-war – against each other in the Colosseum to celebrate Rome's millennium.

He is also thought to have staged a naval battle, for all the world like Caesar or Augustus, on the *naumachia* which Nero constructed at the Vatican.

This was exceptional, for by now the arena seems to have become formalized; throughout the Empire it was an institution, part of the familiar ritual of the Roman government. We know that the Colosseum was carefully rebuilt after the fire at the end of the second century and that it functioned regularly throughout the century that followed. But there is an extraordinary dearth of records and of references to it now, suggesting that it offered few fresh novelties. The four great gladiator schools of Rome were still producing gladiators throughout this period; the trade in beasts – far more extended now with the retreating wilderness – was still gathering exotic animals for Rome from beyond the frontiers. But the great shows of Rome seem to have shared in the stagnation which they had helped produce.

Not that the taste of the populace for regular spectacles had in any way declined. Quite the reverse. According to Burckhardt, writing about the fourth century, 'the Romans were altogether insatiable for anything that might be called a spectacle'.

The Emperor Carinus had even gone so far as to suggest covering part of the Capitol with a huge new wooden amphitheatre for them, 'decorating it most sumptuously with precious stones, gold and ivory, and then displaying, among other rarities, mountain goats and hippopotamuses, and presenting fights between bears and seals'.

The memory of Rome's days of grandeur lingered; but they were little more than memories. Carinus never found the time or the resources to implement these lavish plans, and the state subsidies to pay for the shows became increasingly inadequate. But spectacles of some sort had to continue. The populace demanded them – the government still needed them. Under a powerful emperor like Diocletian there could occur a resurgence of *venationes* and gladiatorial combat in the Colosseum, with hordes of prisoners compelled to fight each other in the arena, 'symbolising', as Professor Grant has written, 'the empire's re-emergence from anarchic disruption to the formidable totalitarian machine of late antiquity'. Such shows were largely demonstrations of the Empire's military might and of the emperor's ruthlessness.

At other times the shows were clearly something of a burden for the government. Increasingly the honour (and expense) of providing them was thrust by the emperor on to his officials and wealthier subjects. According to Burckhardt, the spectacles became 'predominantly the affair of wealthy dignitaries who were required to compensate the state in this fashion and to expend their income in return for immunity from taxation'.

Much of the correspondence of Symmachus, Theodosius' wealthy Prefect of the City, went on the poor man's constant worries over the entertainment he could provide. There were now continual problems of importing suitable beasts for his shows. Gladiators were often in short supply, and thirty Saxon prisoners, earmarked to fight in the Colosseum for one of Symmachus' shows, strangled themselves the night before the fight rather than kill each other. 'Evidently no guard, however efficient, can restrain that desperate race,' Symmachus wrote sadly afterwards. Even when he could get the animals he needed, they were often in such bad shape that they were barely worth fighting – bears that arrived in Rome emaciated and weak from their journey, Libyan lions that had been switched in transit, and other animals too old for the arena. Sometimes the Emperor would offer a few elephants after a Persian victory, but this was exceptional.

Outside Rome, the picture was similar. By the beginning of the third century every Roman centre worthy of its name possessed its amphitheatre or converted theatre where combats and *venationes* could be held. According to Friedländer, 'from Jerusalem to Seville, from Scotland to the borders of the Sahara any town of consequence had its annual victims of the arena.'

The pattern of the Colosseum seems to have been repeated everywhere the Romans went. The shows were commonest in places like Provence and Italy where there had been a definite tradition of gladiators since the late Republic. Nîmes and Arles both had their elaborate amphitheatres based on the plan and the proportions of the Colosseum. Asia Minor and North Africa had become addicted to the sport.

The only areas where the gladiatorial show was not totally adopted were in the northern reaches of the Empire and in Greece. In the North, poverty and sparseness of population hindered the full acceptance of the cult, and there are few remains of stone amphitheatres.

In Greece, the traditions of a more humane culture caused some resistance to the gladiators, but even here a taste for them gradually developed. This was a slow process. When the first gladiatorial games were given in Greece by King Antiochus

Epiphanes, there was a strong reaction of disgust, even though he permitted the fights to go no further than a wounding. This changed. Killings were finally permitted. Before long, volunteers were fighting in the arena, and by the end of the first century the Roman colony at Corinth had its own stone amphitheatre – its ruins still exist. Athens followed suit. When Hadrian visited the city he gave a spectacle in the stadium with gladiators and a hundred beasts.

Thus, throughout the Roman provinces, the shows, *venationes* and the gladiatorial fights had virtually become a necessity, paid for by the local aristocracy and wealthier citizens and demanded by the populace. The usual practice was for the priests and magistrates, who held their office for a year, to pay for them, although sometimes quite humble tradesmen on the make would mount a show. Lucretius talks slightingly of an inn-keeper and a cobbler who had the effrontery to organize a show in their provincial town. 'Anyone', wrote Dio of Prusa, 'who would gain popular favour must get not only jugglers, athletes and actors, but a wild lion or a hundred bulls, or even, should he desire to please the mob, the unspeakable thing.' For Dio, sensitive humane Greek that he was, 'the unspeakable thing' meant gladiators.

Dio was exceptional. Even now, when the shows were getting past their prime and becoming an increasing burden to the wealthier classes of the Roman world, the silence of these people on the subject was remarkable. We have already seen how little discomfort the gladiatorial slaughter caused educated Romans at the beginning of the Empire – Cicero stolidly maintaining that the sight of blood would bring a touch of manliness to his effete fellow-citizens, while Seneca's lone voice registered one individual's shocked understanding of what was going on. Seneca had no followers in Nero's Rome. What few objections have survived come not from Roman writers but for the most part from the philosophers of Greece and Asia Minor.

The Greek historian, Plutarch, pointedly advised the governors of towns to abolish gladiatorial combats or, if this was impossible, to do everything they could to limit them. In his book, *Anacharsis*, Lucian condemned gladiatorial fights as 'bestial, crude, harmful' and destructive of the fighting talent that could be better used against Rome's enemies. Lucian also relates how the Greek philosopher, Demonax, had told the Athenians that they should first 'abolish the Altar of Pity' if they intended to emulate Corinth with its amphitheatre. Another

Worshippers of Isis in procession with the sacred symbols of the goddess.

Greek work by an anonymous disciple of Pythagoras contained one of the strongest contemporary attacks on the arena. It was entitled *On the Eating of Flesh*, and like Seneca's letters warned against the effect the shows had on the souls and sensibilities of the spectators. 'The degeneration of taste infected other senses, and the eye no longer took pleasure in dances, pictures and statues, but in death and wounds as the most precious spectacle.' And that was all.

As attempts to stir the conscience of the Graeco-Roman world such protests were pathetic. If emperors like Hadrian and Marcus Aurelius had been unable to retard the Empire-wide momentum of the shows, what hope had a handful of minor philosophers inspired by nothing stronger than the outworn idealism of Greece?

In the absence of any real opposition to the arena, the emergent Christians might have seemed the natural scourge of the Roman games, the one group with sufficient confidence and faith to do what the ancient world had failed so notably to do – to attack the 'unspeakable thing'. As a persecuted minority the Christians were to experience the horror of the arena at first hand. And as exponents of a creed of love and human dignity they might have seemed compelled to oppose a system that cried out against everything they believed in.

Instead, it took a long time for the Christian opposition to the arena to declare itself. Even when it did, there failed to be that head-on confrontation that seemed inevitable. The later legends of the faith were to make so much of the martyrdoms of the arena that it is surprising to discover how little impact the Christians had upon the system of the Roman games and spectacles.

To explain this, one must place the legends of the Christian martyrs of the arena against their background and understand the relationship between this unique religion and the religious ethos of the Empire.

The Roman attitude to all exotic faiths was traditionally one of tolerance. Indeed, in most religious matters Rome was quite staggeringly open-minded, recognizing any people's gods provided they did the same to the gods of Rome. The Roman Pantheon had many mansions. The only change in this policy occurred with the Empire: with the inauguration of the cult of emperor-worship, the recognition of the Roman gods took on political significance. Failure to acknowledge the imperial divinity became a form of treason.

From the outset, the Romans seem to have distrusted the Christian community, sensing, quite rightly, that this strange brand of Judaism was completely different, both in kind and character, from all other sects tolerated within the city. The Christian cells seemed like the secret societies Caesar had once forbidden; their members were for the most part drawn from the classes which the rulers feared might ultimately revolt.

The unrelenting attitudes of the Christians did little to reassure the Romans. Christians objected to holding public office, to performing military service and to offering obeisance to the imperial cult. At times it must have seemed as if they were perversely trying to affront the Romans when they condemned most popular amusements as barbaric. By putting the master and the slave together in their congregations, Christians were offending the current social code. Meeting secretly at night sometimes led to charges of immoral rites and ritualistic murder. Sometimes they were accused of orgies of incest and infanticide. The Christian practice of calling each other 'brother' and 'sister' gave a particularly sinister twist to the rumours; and it was said that they even ate the flesh and drank the blood of a son of man. Their denial of the gods of Rome made people think them atheists, while the Christian longing for the Messiah whose coming would upset the earthly state made them appear subversive revolutionaries.

Thus hatred and mistrust of the Christians were widespread among all classes during the first century. No accusation was too wild to be believed, and the first persecutions of the Christians that began in Rome in Nero's reign almost certainly had a popular origin. Nero then used them to divert the general anger at the burning of the city. This extremist sect offered the government useful scapegoats for the disaster, and the mob spent their anger on them. Tacitus described the scene of these early persecutions of the unfortunate Christians. 'Mockery of every sort was added to their deaths. Covered with the skins of beasts, they were torn by dogs and perished, or were nailed to posts and covered in pitch to serve as a nightly illumination when daylight had expired.'

The Christians were thrown to the beasts in the big wooden amphitheatre Nero built in the Campus Martius; the human torches were set up in the grounds of the Golden House, near the site of the future Colosseum.

At this time the Christians in the Empire were still a small minority, and after Nero's reign the persecutions seem to have died away. During the second century Trajan and Hadrian positively discouraged the hunting down of Christians and imposed penalties on false accusers. As Hadrian wrote in a letter to Minucius Fundanus: 'If anyone prosecutes them and proves them guilty of any illegality, you must pronounce sentence according to the seriousness of the offence. But if anyone starts such proceedings in the hope of financial reward, then for goodness sake arrest him for his shabby trick and see that he gets his deserts.'

Popular antagonism remained the main cause of persecutions until the reign of Marcus Aurelius. Then suddenly the situation changed. Alarmed by the growing power and numbers of the Christians, the Roman state passed to the defensive. The persecutions started to be organized. Refusal to acknowledge the imperial divinity was enforced now as a capital crime, and for the first time Christians throughout the Empire had to face the likelihood of martyrdom as one of the hazards of their faith. As the great Tertullian exclaimed: 'The outcry is that the state is filled with Christians, that they are in the fields, in the citadels, in the islands; they make lamentation, as for some calamity, that both sexes, every age and condition, even high rank, are passing over to the profession of the Christian faith.'

Between the impassioned certainties of a much later age of faith and the strange dearth of almost all reliable contemporary records, it is an uphill task to start to calculate the size, the scale and the form of Christian suffering during the persecutions. It is still harder to be certain whether any Christians suffered in the Colosseum. The main sources of our information on the Christian persecutions are the *Church History* by Eusebius and Lactantius' pamphlet, *de Mortibus Persecutorum*. Neither is complete and the evidence they offer is often suspect or completely contradictory. According to Tertullian, for instance, a hundred Christians were martyred during a single day in Egypt, whereas in Palestine not more than a hundred martyrs were put to death during all the years of persecution. In Phrygia, Eusebius describes a whole town burned for professing Christianity. As for what went on in Rome, he is silent.

Certainly, it seems that some Christians, in the Roman provinces at least, ended their days in the arena. Eusebius describes the slaughter of four martyrs of the Gallic Church.

Maturus, Sanctus, Blandina and Attalus were taken to the amphitheatre to face the wild beasts and to furnish open proof of the inhumanity of the heathen, the day of fighting wild beasts being purposely arranged for our people. They ran the gauntlet of whips, in accordance with the local custom, they were mauled by the beasts and endured every torment that the frenzied mob on one side or the other demanded and howled for, culminating with the iron chain that singed the flesh and suffocated them by the neck. In the end they were sacrificed after being made a day-long spectacle in place of the normal gladiatorial shows.

There is also evidence that St Perpetus and St Felicitas were thrown to the beasts at Carthage at the end of the second century. According to the account, the beasts were erratic executioners and both saints had to be finished off with the sword. There is also an account, generally taken to have been by an eyewitness, of the martyrdoms of Thanacus Probus and Andronicus in another provincial amphitheatre. This has come down to us from Felix and Verus Macarius and has about it a certain ring of truth.

The wild beasts were let loose, especially a very frightened bear; then a lioness. Both roared fearfully at each other but did not attack the martyrs, much less devour them. The master of the games became enraged and ordered the spearmen to kill them. The bear was pierced through, but the lioness made her escape through an open door. Then Maximus commanded the gladiators to kill the Christians. When this was done, Maximus told ten soldiers to mutilate the two martyrs so that the Christians could not tell them apart.

It is hard to know how many other Christians met their end like this throughout the Empire. Certainly the numbers were exaggerated in later devotional and propagandist works. But just as certainly other devoted Christians must have met this fate in the provinces during the two main persecutions – under Marcus Aurelius and Diocletian. As we have seen, there was a long tradition of employing the beasts of the arena as executioners of the worst criminals: Christians were often thought doubly dangerous, being guilty of both treason to the state and magical practices. Furthermore, the expanding Christian community

The legends of martyrdom in the Colosseum caught in the imagination of the Counter-Reformation. This painting by Juan de las Roelas (*c.* 1560–1625) links the death in the arena of St Ignatius of Antioch (seen in the detail above) with St Ignatius Loyola, founder of the Jesuits.

served as the scapegoats of the Roman world, just like the Jews in Nazi Germany. As Tertullian wrote: 'If Tiber overflows and Nile does not; if Heaven stands still and withholds its rain and the earth quakes, if famine or pestilence take their marches through the country, the word is, "Away with these Christians to the lions".'

And what of the Colosseum? Were these same words uttered in Rome, and were the same scenes re-enacted in its vast arena?

Certainly the later myths and legends of the saints insist that they were. One could construct a fearsome catalogue of bestial depravity supposedly committed on the holy bodies of the faithful inside the Colosseum. Many such legends are concerned with the death of St Ignatius of Antioch, who in the year 160 was supposedly brought from Antioch to Rome to meet death in the arena. In the accounts – there are at least five of them – Ignatius was an eager martyr who actually begged the Roman people not to deprive him of the crown of martyrdom by granting him freedom in the ring. In his so-called 'Letter to the Romans', Ignatius seems to have been drawn by the horror of the arena.

> All the way from Syria to Rome I am fighting with wild animals on land and sea, by night and day, fettered to ten leopards – a squad of soldiers – whom kindness makes even worse. May it be for my own good that the wild animals are ready for me. I pray that I may find them prompt. . . . Come fire and cross and grappling with wild beasts, cuttings and manglings, wrenching of bones, breaking of limbs, crushing of my whole body; come cruel fortune of the devil to assail me. Only be it minutes to attain unto Jesus Christ.

This is the authentic language, not of contemporary persecution, but of the sort of high-flown devotional excess which Christian martyrs unfailingly inspired in later writers. The actual evidence is far too thin to allow Ignatius to take his place among the gladiators, prisoners-of-war and criminals who died in the arena: even more so with the most celebrated of the legendary martyrs of the Colosseum, St Eustace. This was the centurion of the Emperor Hadrian who, according to a seventh-century legend, was converted by a vision of a stag with Christ crucified between its antlers. According to this legend, he and his family were thrown to the beasts of the arena who refused to touch them. Finally the Emperor ordered them to be cooked alive inside the bronze figure of a bull. But again the evidence of Eustace's martyrdom in the Colosseum has been discounted by the strictest Christian scholarship. Similarly with all that colourful band of saintly martyrs who allegedly met their maker after the torments of the Colosseum: St Eleuterio, who was supposedly offered to a lion and lioness who refrained from harming him, St Allesandro, who also emerged unscathed from the arena and had to be beheaded, and the noble virgin, Taziana, who, when offered to a lion, inspired the animal to pay homage at her feet.

Colossal head of the Emperor Constantine.

The more prosaic truth appears to be that, while Christians were undoubtedly persecuted – and even executed – at Rome, there is no direct evidence of a single death in the arena of the Colosseum. One may have happened, but on several counts it seems unlikely. In the first place, it is known that, compared with the Roman provinces – Africa in particular – Rome never saw the worst excesses of the Christian persecutions. In the second, the choice of victims for the Colosseum was never in the hands of the sort of petty local magistrates and priests who in a small provincial town could have been swayed by the demands of an anti-Christian mob. And thirdly, the normal way of executing Christians in the city was by beheading, by the public executioner, at the official place of death, the Ager Esquilinus.

It would be pleasing to believe that the Christian spirit worked to arouse the conscience of the pagan world against the cruelty and inhumanity of the arena. That it did so was certainly suggested by the cult of martyrs for so long associated with the Colosseum. It also might appear self-evident from the way in which the Emperor Constantine in 326 finally banned the gladiatorial shows throughout the Empire after his conversion to Christianity in the year 312. Certainly there was a profound connection between the arena and the early Christians. What is debatable is whether it was quite as simple as it appears.

It was Gibbon who pointed out the curious obsession of many early Christians with the drama of martyrdom and in particular with the horrors of the arena. Before the third century the young Christian Church had wisely but uncourageously kept clear of the arena and all its works. To quote Tertullian again: 'We do not frequent the circus, the theatre, the arena, and have no delight in your barbarous practices. We are utter strangers to the atrocities and follies in which you delight. But the loss, if loss there be in such madness, is ours, not yours, and surely we may be allowed the liberty of differing in taste from you.'

There is an echo of this attitude in St Augustine's celebrated account of the Christian Alypius' visit to the arena and the disastrous effect the sight of blood had upon his soul (page 16).

St Augustine. He warned against those spiritual dangers of the arena to which so many other Christians succumbed.

Both Tertullian and Augustine seem to have had a real awareness of the nature and the danger of the arena. Both knew its power and its importance to the Roman state. And both were supremely anxious to keep the faithful uncontaminated with its influence. The arena was the centre of the mass state ritual of Rome. It brought the pagan gods to the urban masses of the Empire. With its hysteria, its sacrifice, and the presence of the effigies of pagan gods and even of the deified emperor, the arena was a form of anti-religion for the early Christians. It was the seat of anti-Christ and the home of the devil.

There could be no greater contrast than between Augustine's attitude and that ascribed to the martyr, Ignatius. Augustine wanted to keep clear of the arena. Ignatius longed to join it – as a victim. Augustine knew the dangers. Ignatius demonstrated them. In his 'Letter to the Romans', and in the writings and effusions of many later martyrs and would-be martyrs, one cannot avoid the sense of hideous excitement cast on these Christians by the arena. According to Friedländer: 'Only very slowly and gradually did Christianity succeed in weaning the ancient world from the bloodshed of the arena. Very many Christians frequented it, and their imagination was stirred by it.' For the Christians, the arena could easily become the place where they could feel themselves sharing Christ's agony. Here the whole morbid, masochistic element in Rome's death-shows could cast its spell on the all too ready consciences of Christians. Here they could bear their witness to the faith; here they could joyfully tread their own *via crucis*, in the belief that they would surely enter heaven.

This was contagious. Gibbon quotes the remark by Sulpicius Severus, according to whom Christians were 'desiring martyrdom with more eagerness than his contemporaries solicited a bishopric'. Occasionally the state was embarrassed by this collective death-wish. Shocked by the Christians seeking martyrdom, Antoninus Pius cried, 'Unhappy men! If you are thus weary of your lives is it so difficult for you to find ropes and precipices?'

As Augustine knew, the arena was a danger to the Church, but not primarily as a source of persecution. The real threat came from its infection. One of the most terrible of the visions that tempted St Hilarion in the desert with the desires of the flesh was an armed charioteer who sprang on his back and rode him like a horse. In another the saint was actually fighting in the arena. One of the gladiators fell at his feet begging him to bury him.

The truth was that the bloodshed and horror of the arena gripped the imagination of the persecuted Christians. Far from their consciences rebelling, they often found themselves drawn irresistibly towards this point of slaughter. The power of the arena helped to fuel the whole cult of martyrs.

The ambivalence of many of the early Christians to the arena helps to explain their inconsistency during the final phases of the great spectacles of the Empire. Certain important Christian writers – most notably Tertullian and Augustine – were whole-heartedly and consistently opposed to them. Others were not. Even Constantine, the first Christian emperor and the man credited with abolishing gladiatorial games in the Empire, was notably half-hearted on the subject. His edict abolishing the combats was issued from Berytus (Beirut) in 326, almost certainly in response to pressure from certain fathers of the Church assembled at the Council of Nicaea. Certainly it was not prompted by any sense of Christian pity in that most calculating emperor's breast; his edict went on to state that criminals who previously would have endured the chances of the gladiator schools would henceforth face the certain death of forced labour in the mines. Nor can it have been produced by any strongly held belief in the inherent evil of the shows. Constantine had always been keen on the arena. Not long before the edict of Beirut he cheerfully condemned a mass of German prisoners to the swords of the imperial gladiators. A few months *after*, he was writing to the Umbrian town of Hispellum sanctioning gladiatorial shows and actually suggesting that the local priests join forces for a combined show at Bolsena. There is evidence that thirty years later – by then Christianity had been the official religion of the Empire for over forty years – the quaestors at Rome were still offering gladiatorial combats in their December games.

Antoninus Pius, who was shocked by the collective death-wish of the Christians.

In fact, the ending of the Roman spectacles was a gradual process. There are no signs of any tidal wave of outraged Christian feeling sweeping them away, as some writers seem to have imagined. The end of the arena was at best a very partial victory for the faith. It was the economic burden of the games, the shortage of trained gladiators within the collapsing Empire, that basically destroyed the gladiatorial shows. Not conscience but hard economics finally stamped out the 'unspeakable thing'. The Christian protest was at best a convenient excuse for the authorities to ban what they could no longer pay for.

The last gladiatorial combats in the Eastern Empire seem to have taken place towards the year 400 – in the West they

Spoil-sport – the Emperor Honorius, who closed down the last of Rome's gladiator schools.

continued slightly longer. There, mindful of the reactions of the mob, the Emperor Honorius proceeded warily. In 399 he closed down the remaining gladiator schools. By this time gladiatorial combats within the Colosseum must have become a rarity. For more than a century the tendency had been towards staging *venationes* and occasional mass battles waged with barely trained prisoners-of-war. And then, in the year 404, the Colosseum was the scene of the bizarre event which was to mark the definitive end of the whole cult of the gladiators in Rome. Telemachus, a monk from Asia Minor, rushed into the arena and with the same fanaticism that had prompted earlier Christians to beg for martyrdom attempted to separate the gladiators. Not to be cheated of the sight of blood, the crowd tore him to pieces. Honorius responded by abolishing the gladiators and their games for ever. Even so, the *venationes* lingered on in Rome and in the Empire. Alaric, the first barbarian conqueror of Rome, entered and sacked the city in the year 410. *Venationes* of a sort continued, nothing elaborate by now. The ruined city could not afford the excess and splendour of the great days of the Empire. But animals were still paraded in the Colosseum; hunters still marched against them; and these crowds in the twilight of the Roman Empire found, as they always had, excitement and release from the world's reality in these last threadbare shows within Vespasian's masterpiece. As the barbarians marched unhindered through the city, the only blood the Romans shed was in the Colosseum.

The Colosseum as religious monument. Pope Paul VI leading the annual Good Friday procession on its route past the Colosseum.

# Epilogue

Gold seal of the twelfth-century Emperor Frederick Barbarossa.

The Roman Empire fell, but not the Colosseum. It was more durable than the world that had created it. It could be pillaged, not destroyed. In a world grown petty it possessed the super-human scale of the age that built it. To demolish it would have required a confidence and sense of purpose which vanished with the Empire.

Functionally, it did die, although the memory of the *venationes* lingered on among the barbarian 'kings' of Rome; *venationes* were occasionally revived until the end of the seventh century. For practical purposes, Rome had become one of the world's backwaters. Ruined, half-forgotten, it had ceased to be the head of what remained of the Western Empire. And yet Theodoric the Goth managed to stage some sort of hunt in the Colosseum as part of his attempt to imitate what was remembered of the splendour of the emperors. When his son-in-law, Eutarico, had himself grandiloquently proclaimed consul, he too considered it incumbent upon him to provide a show in the Colosseum. It was apparently no great success. Theodoric suggested that next time he should pay the huntsmen more. There was no next time. The shows were over. Ancient Rome was dead. For several centuries the Colosseum slipped into the obscurity which shrouded the greatest city of antiquity.

During these lost years – from the seventh to the eleventh centuries – the first stage of despoilment took place. The cellars under the arena filled with debris. The marble 'thrones' from the *pulvinar* were looted, several ending up as episcopal thrones in Roman churches, where they can be seen today.

The elaborate statuary from the façade and the interior disappeared, much of it to the city's lime-kilns – Romans were fond of using ancient marble as their raw material. The great

The Colosseum of the imagination. Etching by Piranesi of a fantastic Roman prison, from his series *Carceri d'Invenzione*.

bronze fittings and the gilded net encircling the arena had already vanished; soon scavengers would start heaving the iron cramps from the stonework. These had originally been fixed with lead to hold the stones in place. By now Rome had become so backward that even iron was scarce, making it worth the effort of burning them out with sulphur, and so pitting the façade with the great rash of holes one sees today. But such was the skill of Vespasian's masons that this seems not to have affected the Colosseum's stability.

Nor did the damage of these years do anything to impair the extraordinary dual role the Colosseum was beginning to assume. Rather the reverse. The damage merely made it more mysterious, and gradually the Colosseum's double life began. For it was two things now that its active life was over – the greatest surviving ruin in the city, and a testimonial to Rome's imperial past. In the second role, the Colosseum was to become the centre of an ever-changing myth, a symbol for succeeding generations of what they feared and longed for in the history of Rome.

Simply as real estate the Colosseum possessed considerable importance. It was a natural fortress and by the eleventh century had been adroitly occupied by one of the turbulent families controlling Rome. During this period of double-dealing, baronial assertiveness and urban banditry, the dominating families of Rome had started to build themselves fortified redoubts within the surviving masonry of the Empire. The Colonna family had the most impregnable ruin of all – the great tomb of Hadrian beside the Tiber which was to become the Pope's own Castel Sant'Angelo. The Sabelli lived in the Theatre of Marcellus, the Corcites in the Quirinale, and the Frangipane family rapidly consolidated their hold on the Colosseum and the surrounding district.

At the peak of their power, the Frangipane family held the Arch of Titus, seen here in a painting by A.L.R. Ducros, as well as the Colosseum.

It must have been a most impressive fortress, and it could easily have become a key point of the city. During the battles fought between the people and the nobility it changed hands several times. Pope Innocent II, backed by the Frangipane, actually took refuge there from his rival, Anacletus II. In the year 1144, when the Roman people temporarily ejected the feudal families from Rome and tried to set up a Senate on what it thought to be the pattern of the ancient Roman Senate, the Colosseum was one of the first great monuments they occupied. It was officially declared the property of the city.

For by now the myth of the Colosseum had become established. Its uniqueness as a building, its scale and power which once expressed the aspirations of the Flavians, could catch the imagination in a way no other ruin could. It was a living force, at once a challenge and an inspiration from this legendary, superhuman empire from the past.

No other building in the world has been quite as successful in embodying so rich a myth of a whole civilization as the Colosseum. It became a sort of mouthpiece for the past, speaking a multitude of messages to later generations. Already in the eighth century it was being seen as the embodiment of the whole spirit and continuity of Rome. This is expressed in the famous sentence attributed to the Venerable Bede: 'Quamdiu stat Colysaeum stat et Roma, quando cadet Colysaeum cadet et Roma, quando cadet et Roma cadet et mundus' – 'As long as the Colosseum stands, so does Rome. When it falls, Rome falls and the whole world with it.'

The Venerable Bede, the eighth-century monk from Jarrow, England, who wrote the famous *Ecclesiastical History*.

Some of the early Christians had already understood the uncanny way in which the Colosseum stood as a symbol of the Roman Empire. The wise Augustine had tried to insist that the Church should have no connection with the earthly Rome of monuments and the imperial past. The new Rome had to be a Rome of the spirit, freed from the distorting legacy of pagan Rome. Gregory the Great was later to agree with him, and at one point even advocated the destruction of the pagan monuments, including the Colosseum. But it was almost as impossible to do this as to wipe out the whole Roman contribution to Western civilization, and Gregory later changed his mind. As he was to write to Mellito, Abbot of France, the monuments could stay. All that he wanted now was to replace the pagan idols with Christian symbols.

The celebrated medieval guide-book, the *Miribilia Urbis Romae*, written about the year 1000, underlines the way the Colosseum had begun to grow in men's imaginations. By now it was a fabulous affair, no longer an amphitheatre, but the remains of a great temple of the sun and centre of the pagan festivals of Rome. It was believed to have possessed once an enormous gilded dome, destroyed by Pope Silvester when Christianity triumphed over the pagan gods of Rome.

For, like the pyramids, Stonehenge and the Aztec Temples of the Sun, the mere geometry of the Colosseum lent itself to endless speculation. Certain medieval writers traced its groundplan back to the solar wheel; it had been built by Antichrist; it was the 'temple of temples' of pagan Rome, the magic centre of the Empire. Other writers saw it as one of the legendary seven wonders of the world, ascribing its design to Virgil.

The ineradicable legend of martyrdom. Detail of *The Death of St Sebastian* by J. Lieferinxe.

As Michela di Macco points out in her recent book, the Colosseum also became an important political symbol, something of a rallying-point for all who dreamed of reinstating the lost glories of imperial Rome during the later Middle Ages. After the popular revolution of 1144, the so-called 'Senate' set up by the people dutifully took possession of the major Roman monuments and even started to restore them. This was done partly as a pious act, partly as a piece of pure historical nostalgia. By returning to these antique monuments, these twelfth-century Romans dreamed of returning to the splendours of a past when Rome and its citizens had ruled the world. Above all, they rejected the conspiracy of wealthy families who had inherited the city. The Frangipane were accordingly ejected from the Colosseum, which was effectively proclaimed communal property.

In a way, this very act revealed the weakness of the revolutionaries. The Colosseum, more than all the other ruins, was a splendid symbol. But it was hard to see what anyone could do with it, apart from continuing to use it as a fortress. There was obviously no question of restoring it to its original state, much less to its original purpose. In fact the revolutionaries did little, except attempt to remove all signs of the hated Frangipane; and their Senate did not last. In 1159 the Colosseum was a fortress once again and in the hands of the Frangipane. And once again this soon became interpreted as a symbolic act which represented, as nothing else could do, the return of power in Rome to the barons and the Papacy. Soon the Frangipane were adopting the image of the Colosseum as their family device, the emblem which was proudly borne before them at the crowning of a pope. And in the following century, when Frederick Barbarossa again attempted in his struggle with the Pope to revive his version of the Roman Empire, the Colosseum was his symbol too. He put it on his seal and on his banners, signifying his ambition to restore the Golden Age of Rome.

Before this period there was a lone voice, that of the classicist, Maestro Gregorio, begging quite simply that the Colosseum be understood and treated for what it was – not for its political importance, not as the mythical centre of the cult of Antichrist – but as the masterpiece of the age of Vespasian and Titus, 'a place of beauty indescribable'. It was a vain cry. For all except devoted classicists the actual building of the Colosseum scarcely mattered. The idea of studying it, still less of paying money to restore it, would have seemed ridiculous. More than ever, it was the myth that mattered. What could thirteenth-century

Rome do with a building like the Colosseum, except leave it to the poorest prostitutes and evil-livers who used to sleep beneath its arches? Petrarch, who had dreamed of the Colosseum as the crown of Rome, was shocked to find how badly damaged it had been by the earthquake of 1349. None of the damage was made good. The stones were used for other buildings.

With the Renaissance, this contrast between the mythical existence and the reality of the Colosseum becomes, if anything, still more exaggerated. For once again it is a source of vital inspiration – this time to the architects and artists who use it as a touchstone and a document from the great age of Roman architecture which they are planning to bring back to Italy. Brunelleschi and Alberti studied it. In Florence the Palazzo Rucellai – one of the landmarks of Renaissance building – echoed the architectural forms of the external orders of the Colosseum, while in Rome, three important buildings clearly derive directly from the Colosseum's great façade – the courtyard of the Palazzo Venezia (probably designed by Alberti), and the two important loggias in St Peter's and St Mark's. In turn, the influence of the Colosseum can then be traced in later buildings such as the Cancelleria, the Palazzo Farnese and the great library of the Palazzo della Sapienza.

And yet this period, in which the Colosseum had become something of an architectural ideal, also saw the greatest damage to its fabric. The more the builders copied it, the worse they treated it. Often it was used as a quarry for the very buildings it had inspired. Despite complaints from humanists like Poggio Bracciolini, throughout the Roman building-registers of the fifteenth century the ominous phrase recurs time and again: 'a cavar marmi a coliseo' – 'for removing marble from the Colosseum'. The steps of St Peter's and part of the piazza were built with it; its stone was also used for the Palazzo Venezia, the Palazzo di San Marco and the Cancelleria. Apparently the Colosseum was still the haunt of beggars, brigands, undesirables, and in the popular imagination it remained the undoubted haunt of the devil. The 'temple of temples', it was rich in evil spirits, and it was here that Benvenuto Cellini and a Sicilian priest are supposed to have invoked the forces of the underworld. In his memoirs Cellini graphically described the way the priest drew a magic circle in the arena, and how whole legions of devils soon surrounded them, shrieking and framed in fire, 'so that the whole Colosseum seemed to be burning'.

The Colosseum continued to be a source of inspiration to architects and mathematicians. Title-page from *Antiquarie Prospettiche Romane*, published in about 1500. In later centuries it came to be seen as part of a Roman never-never land. Detail from *Capriccio with Colosseum*, 1745 (*below*).

(*Above*) Pieter Brueghel, *The Tower of Babel* (1563), a Colosseum run to seed.

(*Right*) the loggia of St Peter's, Rome, echoing the arches of the Colosseum.

(*Opposite*) two seminal Renaissance buildings, Alberti's Palazzo Rucellai in Florence and, in Rome, Sangallo's Palazzo Farnese. Yet the building which inspired them was mouldering away, as Heemskerk's *Self-Portrait with Colosseum* (1553) shows *(opposite above)*.

Martijn Van heemskerck
1553

The Colosseum, quarry of Renaissance Rome. (*Above*) stone is dragged away to build Pope Urban VIII's Palazzo Barberini (*left*).

(*Left*) part of St Peter's Square, the paving-stones of which are thought to have been taken from the Colosseum.

(*Opposite*) the Colosseum as it might have been. Fontana's plan, put forward in 1725, for transforming the Colosseum into a martyrs' church.

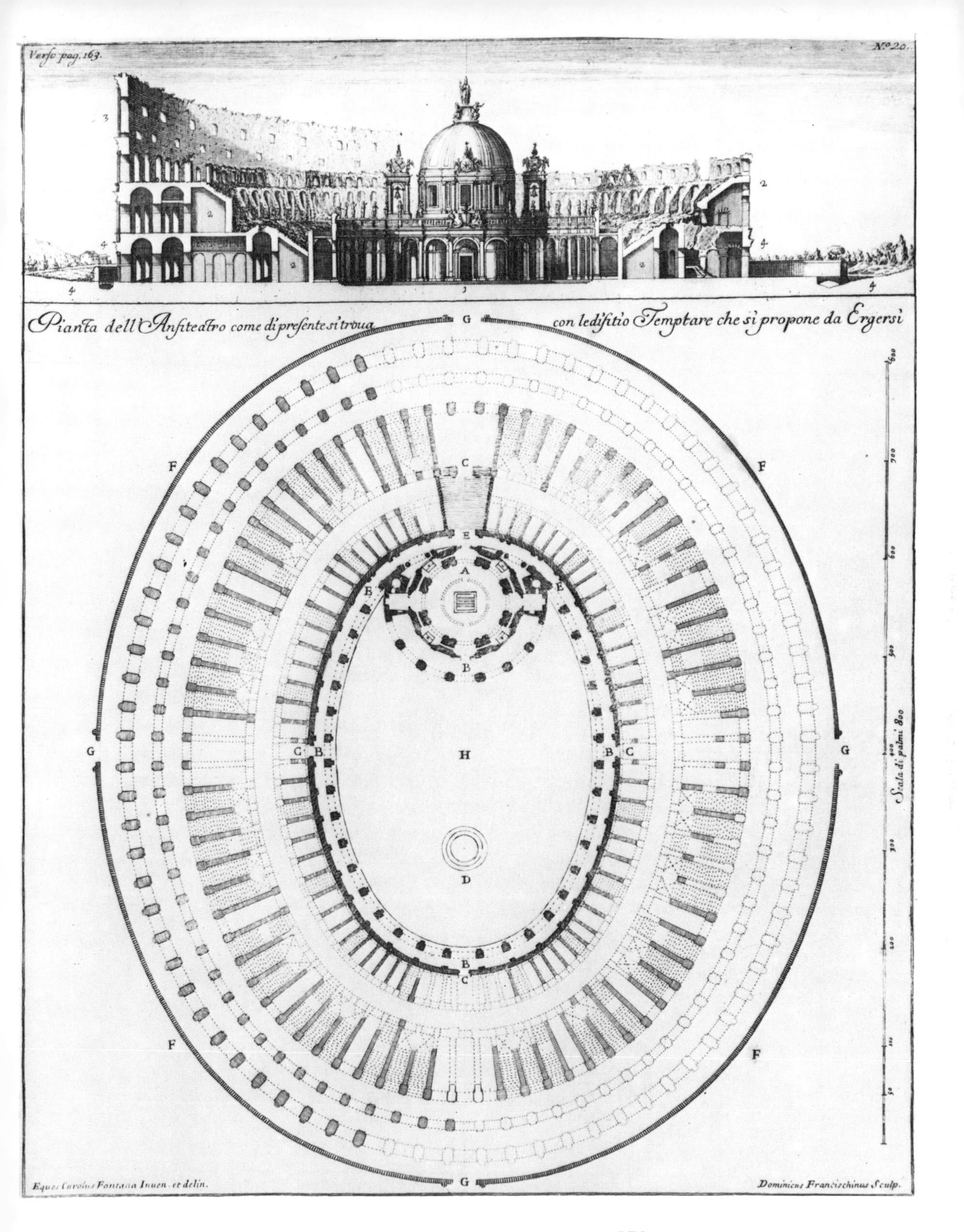
Verso pag. 163.
N.° 20.
Pianta dell'Anfiteatro come di presente si troua
con l'edifitio Temptare che si propone da Ergersi
Scala di palmi 800
Eques Carolus Fontana Inuen. et delin.
Dominicus Franciscinus Sculp.

With such a reputation, the enormous ruin was something of an embarrassment to the authorities. More than ever it was a problem to know what to do with it. Its disreputable condition even conflicted with the splendid city the Renaissance popes were passionately rebuilding by the Tiber. And so the supreme paradox of the Colosseum started. At the point when its aesthetic influence was at its height, it was being systematically ransacked and destroyed. The paradox continued with its preservation. Before the classically inspired Renaissance builders could finally destroy it, another myth came to the rescue. The Counter-Reformation had begun. A new mood of passionate belief and suffering for the faith was sweeping through the Church. Throughout the Roman Catholic world men were laying down their lives for their beliefs. The heroic cult of the Christian martyrs started in earnest.

As we have seen, the evidence of any actual martyrdom within the Colosseum was non-existent. This was no problem to an age of faith. The Colosseum smelt of death. It was the perfect setting for an awesome Christian drama. There were the legendary sixth-century *Acta Martyrum* – a highly coloured and contentious list of mythical figures who had supposedly died for the faith, several of them in the Colosseum: St Ignatius, St Genesius, the actor-saint, St Sebastian, who supposedly suffered in the arena before being shot to death (to the lasting inspiration of Renaissance painters) by a company of archers. The Colosseum started its new life as the centre of a cult. Shrines and a small chapel were built in the arena. Great Christian dramas were staged here by the popes. Sixtus V planned to make the Colosseum a permanent place of worship, but died before he could raise the money – he also had somewhat contradictory plans to turn it into an enormous papal silk factory, complete with a special upstairs storey for the weavers. And the whole movement to make the Colosseum a place of permanent devotion reached its peak in the mid-seventeenth century, when Bernini was commissioned to transform the amphitheatre into a martyrs' temple.

As with everything Bernini touched, his plan was on the grandest scale. Fresh entrances and classical façades would have been built to express the Colosseum's Christian character. Pictures and inscriptions would have been added to emphasize the cult of martyrs, and a high altar raised in the centre of the arena. Just as Michelangelo had converted the great baths of Diocletian into the soaring Church of Santa Maria degli Angeli, so Bernini would have adapted the Colosseum into a still vaster

The interior of the Colosseum as Piranesi saw it in the eighteenth century, a symbol of romantic melancholy.

Christian church. The mind boggles at the result. It was prevented for the usual reason – lack of money – and to do something with the ruin, which was becoming now a place of scandal, Clement X finally walled up the arches to the first storey, and erected a great wooden cross on the walls.

And so the Colosseum more or less survived into an age which could appreciate it without wanting to destroy it. For the eighteenth-century travellers on their grand tours, the Colosseum became part of the essential background of the city. It was scenery, one of the key sights of Rome, a place to wander in, to muse upon the past in. Once more it was a sort of symbol of the city – painted endlessly in eighteenth-century views of Rome – and it began to speak yet another message to these wealthy foreigners: the passing of the power of empires, and the ultimate decay of even the most ambitious human enterprises. This was an age that loved a ruin, so that the additional decay of the previous hundred years gave it an added melancholy and attractiveness. It was decaying, tragic, picturesque, and for the romantic travellers of the turn of the century it was irresistible.

The Colosseum was of course a 'must' for the rich foreigners who flocked to Rome as the culmination of the 'Grand Tour'. The third Duke of Beaufort (*left*) even had his portrait painted by Trevisani with it in the background. Less wealthy travellers took back such popular coloured prints as this eighteenth-century view (*below*).

The Colosseum owed its popularity among the Romantics not least to Goethe, who is seen (*left*) sketching in Rome during his first Italian Journey in 1786. (*Above*) the interior of the Colosseum, complete with hermit, as it was about the time Goethe saw it.

Collapsing, overgrown, containing the small Chapel of Santa Maria della Pieta nel Colosseo with its solitary hermit, the Colosseum became Byron's 'Noble wreck in ruinous perfection'. He loved it and was appalled by it. This was legitimate Byronic territory, and the great myth-maker began to forge yet another myth which was to captivate a succession of romantic travellers throughout the years to come.

> But here, where Murder breathed her bloody steam;
> And here, where buzzing nations choked the ways
> And roar'd or murmur'd like a mountain stream
> Dashing or winding as its torrent strays;
> Here, where the Roman million's blame or praise
> Was death or life, the playthings of a crowd. . . .
>
> But when the rising moon begins to climb
> Its topmost arch, and gently pauses there;
> When the stars twinkle through the loops of time,
> And the low night-breeze waves along the air
> The garland-forest, which the gray walls wear,
> Like laurels on the bald first Caesar's head;
> When the light shines serene but doth not glare,
> Then in this magic circle raise the dead:
> Heroes have trod this spot – 'tis on their dust ye tread.

To be fair, it was Goethe who had really set the fashion for this moonlight viewing of the Colosseum. In his *Italian Journey* for 1787, he described with somewhat self-conscious, painterly skill how he visited it one 'clear and glorious' night.

> The Colosseum looked especially beautiful. It is closed at night. A hermit lives in a small chapel, and some beggars have made themselves at home in the crumbling vaults. These had built a fire on the level ground, and a gentle breeze had driven the smoke into the arena, so that the lower parts of the ruins were veiled and only the huge masses above loomed out of the darkness. We stood at the railing and watched, while over our heads the moon stood high and serene. By degrees the smoke crept through holes and crannies, and in the moonlight it looked like fog. It was a marvellous sight.

Madame de Staël followed his example and was duly impressed. So was Stendhal, who not only went by moonlight, but read Byron too in the arena. Under such influences he found that the immensity of the Colosseum suggested 'not an elegy, but a great sublime tragedy'.

During the years of the romantic travellers the Colosseum found its ideal modern role. It was the perfect tourist spot, the most sublime romantic ruin in the world. For many years the

Turner's impression of the Colosseum by moonlight – by now a cliché of the Roman itinerary.

Camera Apostolica had the sense to try to preserve it exactly as it was – even to facilitate these celebrated moonlight tours by wealthy foreigners. Picturesque beggars, overgrown decay, even a broken pillar on which to sit, like Stendhal, reading one's Byron: it was too good to last. Such an important monument had to be restored – and was, somewhat heavy-handedly, by Canina, Folchi and Poletti during the 1840s. The ruined inner southern wall was neatly, incongruously, rebuilt, and an inscription placed upon it recording the munificence of Pope Gregory XVI.

None of this prevented the Colosseum from being lit by Bengal lights to honour first the election of Pope Pius IX in 1846, and later to celebrate the arrival of his deadly enemy, the short-lived Roman Republic. But before long the picturesque yielded yet further to reality. As we have seen, the foliage and undergrowth that Byron loved had to give way to the demands of the archaeologists. Excavation before inspiration. The chapel went – so did the shrines, the romantic bric-à-brac and masonry, the beggars, the Stations of the Cross. The Colosseum found itself shaved, scoured, stripped of the accretions of the centuries. Finally the Fascists in the 1920s completed this exercise in nudity by clearing the whole area beyond the Forum and building a wide new boulevard in honour of Mussolini's Empire. It was

Since Mussolini cleared the buildings round it, the Colosseum has stood beleaguered and alone, its stonework threatened by pollution and the vibration of the traffic.

the Duce's aim to open up the city, with immense vistas swathing through the poorer quarters, rather as Baron Haussmann's boulevards had been built in Paris. One of the few places where he succeeded was round the Colosseum. Its cushion of medieval buildings and the gardens and orchards of the Oppio were lost. Vespasian's amphitheatre was finally exposed, purposeless and bare, devoid even of the myths and misunderstandings that had been clustering round it since the Roman Empire fell. As one Italian writer put it, it was now no more than 'a gigantic traffic island' in a busy city.

But if the myths must go, it would be wrong to overlook the truth about the Colosseum. This is no ordinary ruin: there is no other ancient building in the world with quite such relevance to the late twentieth century. In an uncanny way, the Colosseum and its complex rituals seem to have anticipated developments within our own time.

Vespasian's Rome was a mass society devoid of mass communications. The Colosseum and Rome's amphitheatres and circuses were designed for the sort of popular participation in events that we achieve through television and the cinema and radio. True, we have split up and specialized the various activities which in the Colosseum were confined to one arena, but apart from this the actual activities are similar. We, like the Romans, have once again become a spectator civilization. Like them we have our obsessive sports events, mass rallies, personality cults and secular religions. We have our periods of national hysteria. We even share their interest in violent death, except that, grown more squeamish, we indulge it usually at second hand in films, television reports and novels. It was calculated recently that by the age of twenty the average American male will have witnessed fifteen thousand violent deaths on television alone.

What makes the Roman Colosseum so important is that in some respects it carried these facets of our society to their logical conclusion. With their passion for organization and concern with power, the Romans showed how all these tendencies could be exploited to form a pattern for mass government throughout the Empire. In various respects they went further than we seem prepared to go. With the wealth of the Empire and its slave economy, Rome had reached a level of leisure which America will probably achieve by the end of the century. As for the violence of the arena, it is important to remember how little real resistance the supposedly enlightened Greeks made to the encroaching Roman barbarism.

Apart from this, it seems that we are rapidly employing much the same means as the Romans towards much the same ends. The Colosseum was at the centre of an effective system of empire-wide mass anaesthesia. Over the generations it corrupted and then drained away just those activities making for movement, change, unrest or ambition in society. It substituted ritualized mass fantasies for the realities of politics, religion, self-aggrandizement and war. And in doing so, it helped to turn the exuberant Republic into the deferential empire of Augustus, and finally into the static, stagnant universal state, far more concerned with watching the arena than with repelling the barbarians at its gates.

*The Last Prayer of the Christian Martyrs.* Detail of a painting by Jean Léon Gérôme (1824–1904).

# Further Reading


J. Carcopino, *Daily Life in Ancient Rome*, Harmondsworth, 1970

S. Dill, *Roman Society from Nero to Marcus Aurelius*, London, 1904

D.R. Dudley, *Urbs Roma*, London, 1967

A. Duggan, *Julius Caesar*, London, 1966

D. Earl, *The Moral and Political Tradition of Rome*, London, 1967

L. Friedländer, *Roman Life and Manners under the Early Empire*, London, 1908–13

E. Gibbon, *The Decline and Fall of the Roman Empire*, volume 2, chapter XV, Harmondsworth, 1963, and numerous other editions

M. Grant, *Gladiators*, London, 1967

B.W. Henderson, *The Life and Principate of the Emperor Nero*, London, 1903

T.R. Holmes, *The Roman Republic*, London, 1923

J.H. Huizinga, *Homo Ludens*, London, 1970

G. Jennison, *Animals for Show and Pleasure in Ancient Rome*, Manchester, 1937

R.A. Lanciani, *Ancient Rome*, London, 1967

A.W. Lintott, *Violence in Republican Rome*, London, 1968

T. Mommsen, *The History of Rome*, London, 1960

L. Mumford, *The City in History*, Harmondsworth, 1961

U.E. Paoli, *Rome. Its People, Life and Customs*, London, 1963

M. Rostovzeff, *Rome*, New York, 1960

M.R. Scherer, *Marvels of Ancient Rome*, London, 1955

M. Wheeler, *Roman Art and Architecture*, London, 1964


The writings of Cicero, Marcus Aurelius, Seneca, Suetonius and Tacitus are also of interest and relevance.

# Acknowledgments

Adamklissi Museum 149; Alinari 24, 47, 140 (*top*), 144; Aosta Cathedral 168; Ashmolean Museum, Oxford 175; Azienda di Turismo, Piazza Armerina 121; Badminton, Gloucestershire 182 (*top*); Roloff Beny 154; Bibliothèque Nationale, Paris 156; British Museum, London 1, 6, 7, 10 (*bottom*), 15 (*right*), 20, 21, 25, 31, 42 (*bottom*), 43 (*bottom*), 45, 54, 59 (*bottom*), 64, 68, 69, 93, 97, 99, 104, 105, 111, 115, 120, 133, 140 (*bottom*), 143, 145, 153, 155, 173, 178, 181, 185; Brompton Studio 67; Peter Clayton 115; Controller of Her Majesty's Stationery Office 138 (*bottom*); Courtauld Institute, London 170, 172, 182 (*top*); Fitzwilliam Museum, Cambridge 177 (*top*); Fototeca Unione 10 (*top*), 122; Ray Gardner 1, 7, 54, 68, 120, 133, 143, 155; German Archaeological Institute 38, 66, 102–3, 109, 134; Giraudon 113; Goethe Museum, Düsseldorf 182 (*bottom*), 183 (*bottom*); Italian State Tourist Office 119; John G. Johnson Collection, Philadelphia 174; Keystone Press Agency 169, 186; Kunsthistorisches Museum, Vienna 44, 176 (*top*); Louvre, Paris 24; Mansell-Alinari 11 (*bottom*), 14 (*right*), 28, 29, 33, 42 (*top*), 43 (*top*), 57, 61, 63, 76, 92, 100, 117, 160, 168, 177 (*bottom left*); Mansell-Anderson 9 (*right*), 13, 18, 19, 27, 79, 123; Mansell Collection 23, 37; Georgina Masson 177; Mas 164; Metropolitan Museum, New York 165, 167; Musée des Antiquités, Rouen 12; Musée de Lectoure, Gers 106; Musée Romain, Avenches 96; Museo della Civita Romana, Rome 130–1; Museo dei Conservatori, Rome 140 (*top*); Museums and Art Gallery, Leicester 112; National Museum of Antiquities, Edinburgh 148; Niedersächsisches Staatsarchiv, Wolfenbüttel 171; Ny Carlsberg Glyptotek, Copenhagen 9 (*left*), 53; Josephine Powell 2, 178 (*top, bottom*); Roemerhaus, Augst 58; Oscar Savio 130–1; Edwin Smith 30, 90–1, 101, 114, 138 (*top*), 141; Staatliche Bildstelle, Saarbrücken 14 (*left*), 15 (*left*), 59 (*top*), 116 (*top*), 125; Staatliche Museen, Berlin 85; Statens Museum for Kunst, Copenhagen 183 (*top*); Stourhead, Wiltshire 72; Uffizi, Florence 47; Vatican Museums 11 (*top*), 132, 160, 166, 176 (*bottom*); Walters Art Gallery, Baltimore 187; Roger Wood 128, 129, 139

# Index *Numbers in italics refer to illustrations*